A201

D1798205

CLIMBING AND WALKING IN SOUTH-EAST ENGLAND

By the same author and uniform with this book

A CLIMBER IN THE WEST COUNTRY

CLIMBING
AND WALKING
IN SOUTH-EAST
ENGLAND

by

EDWARD C. PYATT

DAVID & CHARLES
NEWTON ABBOT

0 7153 4878 7

Set in 10 pt on 12 pt Times Roman
and printed in Great Britain
by Clarke, Doble & Brendon Limited
for David & Charles (Publishers) Limited
South Devon House Newton Abbot Devon

CONTENTS

LIST OF ILLUSTRATIONS

7

INTRODUCTION

THE geographical accident which sited the older crag- and mountain-forming rocks to the north and west of England and the newer and softer formations to the south and east has left the south-eastern climber with the considerable problem of how to practise his craft and where to fulfil his mountaineering needs in between trips to real mountains. The many who must live and work in that part of England closest to the Continent find themselves amidst green rounded hills almost completely lacking any exposure of bare rock and faced with travelling long distances to reach more conventional mountaineering scenes.

The climber in Sheffield, say, or Bristol, has climbing rocks within the city boundary and 1,000 ft hills within 20 miles or less. The Lancashire climber poised between North Wales, the Lake District and the Pennines has a tremendous variety of opportunity on his doorstep, so too has the Yorkshireman. The climbers from cities and towns of the South East have but little by comparison. The hills are lower—Walbury Hill in Berkshire at 974 ft is the highest natural elevation within 80 miles of London; it is necessary to say 'natural' because the tower on Leith Hill in Surrey actually reaches 1,000 ft. The nearest 1,000 ft hill is Broadway Hill in the Cotswolds, the nearest 2,000 ft hill a nameless point in the Black Mountains. The highest natural rocks hardly reach 40 ft but there are quarries and sea cliffs that are higher, the latter mostly in gleaming white chalk, the softness of which presents, as we shall see, special problems in climbing. Not only has the south-eastern climber made a great deal out of this unpromising material, but he sits at the centre of a transport network which enables him to go far afield with comparative ease whenever he wishes to do so.

We look then first at the immediate surroundings of the capital, inside a circle of approximately 80 miles radius, the day-trip range, to see what he has contrived for himself therein. We find him walking on the chalk hills of the North and South Downs, the Chilterns and the Downs of Berkshire and Hampshire, on the sandstone hills of the Weald, and on cliff top and beach, alas with only a very limited stretch of unspoilt coastline remaining. He will be found, curiously enough, climbing on chalk on sea cliffs and in quarries, and with great intensity and dedication on a drastically limited amount of sandstone; his caving is in a variety of holes, invariably man-made, in all sorts and conditions of rock.

We look next within a 120-mile circle, the week-end range we may say, where considerable additions to the amenities are found—the sea cliffs and hills of Dorset, the crags, caves and ridges of the Mendip Hills, crags and hills in the Cotswolds, the Forest of Dean and the Malvern Hills, in Worcestershire, Warwickshire and in Charnwood Forest. Even flat East Anglia has some low hills which, just like their bigger brethren, will lure us on to see what is over the far side; hereabouts too the flat coastline, as desolate in its own way as any mountainside, is not without charm. Within this same circle falls that part of the coast of France which lies between Le Havre and Calais, readily accessible in summer months by the frequent cross-channel services. The chalk cliffs here show some striking scenery.

Finally we glance at some of the prospects even further away—brought into the orbit of the south-eastern climber because he is at the hub of the country's transport system of road, rail, sea and air services, namely the Black Mountains and Brecon Beacons, the mountains and crags of North Wales and of the Lake District, the various rocks of Derbyshire and the craggy coastlines of Devon and Cornwall. Certain climbing grounds abroad, too, cannot be considered as out of reach—the climbing at Fontainebleau, south of Paris, and in the Belgian Ardennes is reasonably accessible, while certain Alpine peaks could be ascended in a long week-end by careful planning.

When the sport of mountaineering began in the Alps in the middle of the last century, the south-eastern climber was specially favoured because he was spared a tedious preliminary journey through England on the way to his mountains. Thus the earliest organisation of mountaineers, which became the Alpine Club, was centred from the first on London. Yet few of these early climbers made any attempt to climb or to walk in the South East. Mountaineering meant the Alps and even the British hills were seldom, if ever, visited. As the years went by the possibilities of our home mountains as a practice ground were slowly realised and at Easter and Christmas, parties of climbers went to North Wales and the Lake District where suitable conditions of ice and snow sometimes gave opportunities for sport, having a distinctly Alpine flavour.

Typical of those who conformed to this later pattern was Owen Glynne Jones, that very great all-round climber of the 1890s. He was a schoolmaster who invariably spent his full summer holiday in the Alps, where he climbed with unusual vigour. Off-season he visited the Lake District, making numerous new climbs on all the various crags, and found time to produce his monumental *Rock Climbing in the English Lake District*, the first book to describe climbers' routes on home mountains. There are many legends of his training exploits during his life in London—when Queen Victoria opened the Albert Hall he climbed across the roof to get a better view; he passed round the Common Room at the City of London School without once touching the floor; another climber remembered him backing up the 'chimney' formed by two high parallel brick walls; and so on. He loved to ride on the newly popularised bicycle—to Brighton and back in a day for example—yet he never seems when crossing the Weald to have gone anywhere near the sandstone outcrops, or to have looked at the chalk cliffs so prominent in that part of the south coast.

As we shall see in due course, the story of climbing on these chalk cliffs seems to have gone on without influencing, and without being in any way influenced by, the main stream of climbing in this country. As early as 1858 John Stogdon, later of the Alpine Club, was using chalk to practise for Alpine mountaineering:

> The Hampshire chalk-pits gave fine opportunities for breaking one's neck, and the chalk cliffs of Swanage, Scratchell's Bay, and Beachy Head provided me with quite sensational risks. There are bits on all these places as dangerous as anything in the Alps. To glassade down a steep, hard, chalk slope is not easy, and steps cut in the treacherous, crumbly material are not too reliable. I didn't kill myself, but I had some very close escapes.

In the first sentences of his *Scrambles in the Alps*, Edward Whymper speaks of climbing on Beachy Head in his youth, while a few years later A. F. Mummery, notable Alpine rock climber and mountaineer, used to practise on the chalk cliffs near Dover. Odd climbing activities have continued on Beachy Head as well as on some of the more outstanding cliffs of Kent right up to the present day, while the pinnacles of the Needles off the western tip of the Isle of Wight have also received attention recently.

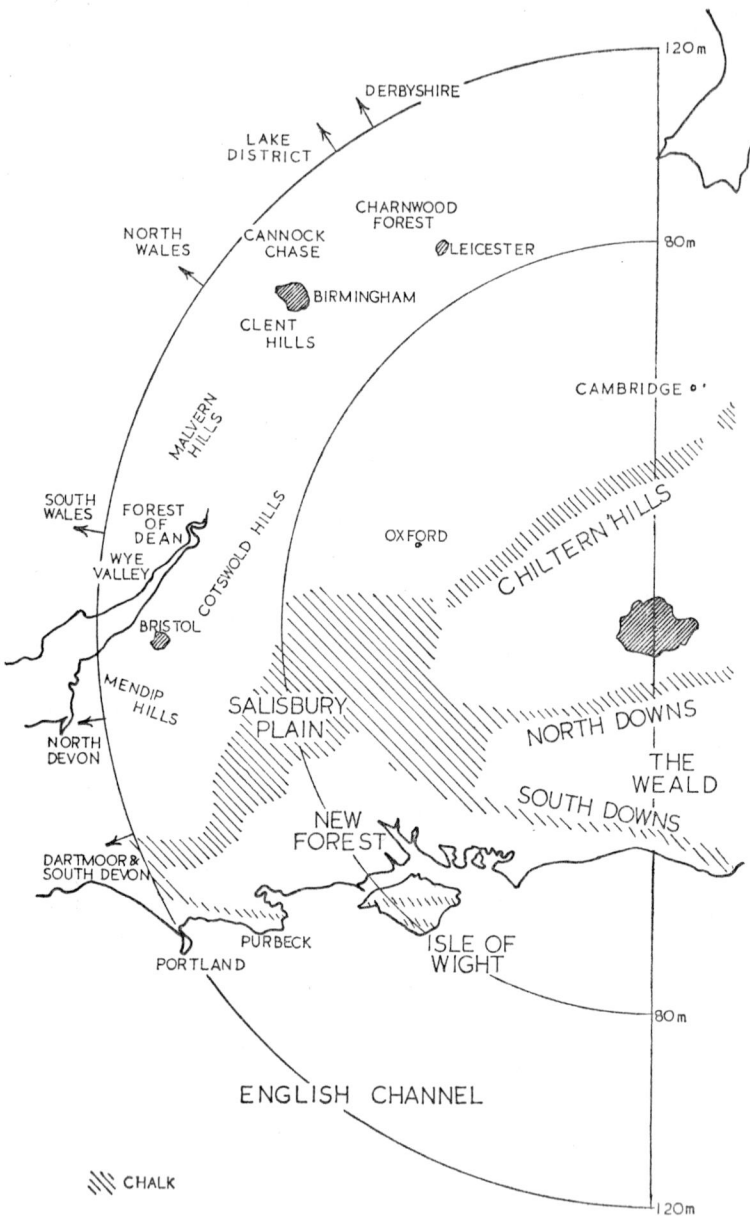

DERBYSHIRE

LAKE
DISTRICT

CHARNWOOD
FOREST

120 m

NORTH
WALES

CANNOCK
CHASE

●LEICESTER

80 m

BIRMINGHAM

CLENT
HILLS

MALVERN
HILLS

CAMBRIDGE ●'

SOUTH
WALES

FOREST
OF
DEAN

COTSWOLD HILLS

OXFORD

CHILTERN HILLS

WYE
VALLEY

BRISTOL

MENDIP
HILLS

SALISBURY
PLAIN

NORTH DOWNS

NORTH
DEVON

THE
WEALD

SOUTH DOWNS

NEW
FOREST

DARTMOOR &
SOUTH DEVON

PURBECK

PORTLAND

ISLE OF
WIGHT

80 m

ENGLISH CHANNEL

120 m

CHALK

Sketch plan centred on London—western sector

The other rock climbing within the 80-mile circle—that on the sandstone of the Weald—only began around 1930. For the first decade progress was slow and delightful. After the war the general upsurge of interest in rock climbing everywhere led to intensification of the attack; with large numbers of participants and only a comparatively small amount of rock, saturation has now been reached. These outcrops represent the ultimate in the divorcement of rock climbing from mountaineering, an evolutionary process which has continued throughout the story of the sport. Originally mountaineering meant the ascent of snow and ice mountains; rocks were sometimes climbed in the course of such expeditions but usually only when they could not be avoided. Rock climbing was thus but a small part of mountaineering. Later rock climbing was developed as a sport in its own right in mountain ranges, such as those of Great Britain, where there is no permanent snow cover. Here only a few mountains are rocky enough to provide climbers' routes from base to summit; on the rest the climbing is done on crag faces which are themselves only comparatively minor features of the mountains from which they rise, and the climbers' route on such a crag cannot in any way be looked upon as a route to the summit of the mountain—the original objective of mountaineering. At first, climbing in British mountains was regarded largely as practice for Alpine mountaineering, but by the 1914–18 war it had progressed so far in the development of its own methods and traditions as to become an independent sport. In the words of an expert of the time: 'British climbing is not undeveloped Alpinism but diverse'.

Just as Alpine mountaineers had benefitted from the use of British hills as practice grounds, so in their turn did British mountain rock climbers look around for training grounds away from mountains, closer to their homes. Thus very early in the story the gritstone edges of the Peak and the Pennines came to be climbed upon at week-ends and the same train of thought brought southern climbers at long last to the sandstone of the Weald in the 1930s. However, while these northern rocks outcrop in an essentially mountain-like setting of wild moorland, their southern counterparts rise among woods and cultivated fields in a comparatively flat land, far removed indeed from the mountains and from the origins of mountaineering.

While the Wealden rocks were first feeling the climbers' tread,

the hill ranges of the south were also beginning to foster some
sort of new feeling towards high places. The hiking movement of
the 1930s led to a vast increase in the use of local hills, not only
by climbers but also by large numbers of other people who found
on elevations like Leith Hill or Box Hill their first taste of mountain atmosphere, of 'earth set on earth a little higher'. Climbing
philosophers began to integrate the whole breadth of mountain
experience from the highest summits of the earth to the lowest of
green and rounded hills, so that Frank Smythe could write:

> Those who love hills need go no higher than Holmbury's summit.
> They will discover there that height counts for little and it is the
> hill that matters.

By such arguments and by energetic pursuit of those things which
are available, we come at last to a local philosophy which discovers
for the southern climber a great deal that is of interest for him to
see and to do.

Of the areas in the 120-mile circle only isolated places have a
record of climbing going back to before the first world war.
Dolomite limestone at Breedon-on-the-Hill in Leicestershire was
climbed upon just before the turn of the century. In the Mendips the
influence of cavers with a climbing background enforced an en-
quiring attitude towards the problems of steep limestone, which led
to climbing in the 1920s, and some scrambles were also done
around the same time in Worcestershire. Everywhere else had to
await the post-war upsurge. What is most surprising of all is that a
fine sea-cliff area like the Dorset coast should have been over-
looked until the late 1950s. Earlier generations of southern climbers were sadly at fault here in turning so readily to chalk, when
they might have exploited the 'tier upon tier of yellow roofs split by
fantastic diedres and chimneys' along the coast of the Isle of
Purbeck.

What is it that a mountaineer seeks in his home countryside
to help him with the whole range of his mountaineering and to
fulfil in between times the basic urges which impel him to the
sport? Clinton Dent, writing in one of the earliest textbooks in
1892, was among the first to suggest an answer:

> A quarry or a chalk-pit may supply his need, an ordinary cross-
> country walk will train his legs, strengthen his ankles, and accustom
> his eyes to localise objects. A ruggedly built railway bridge has

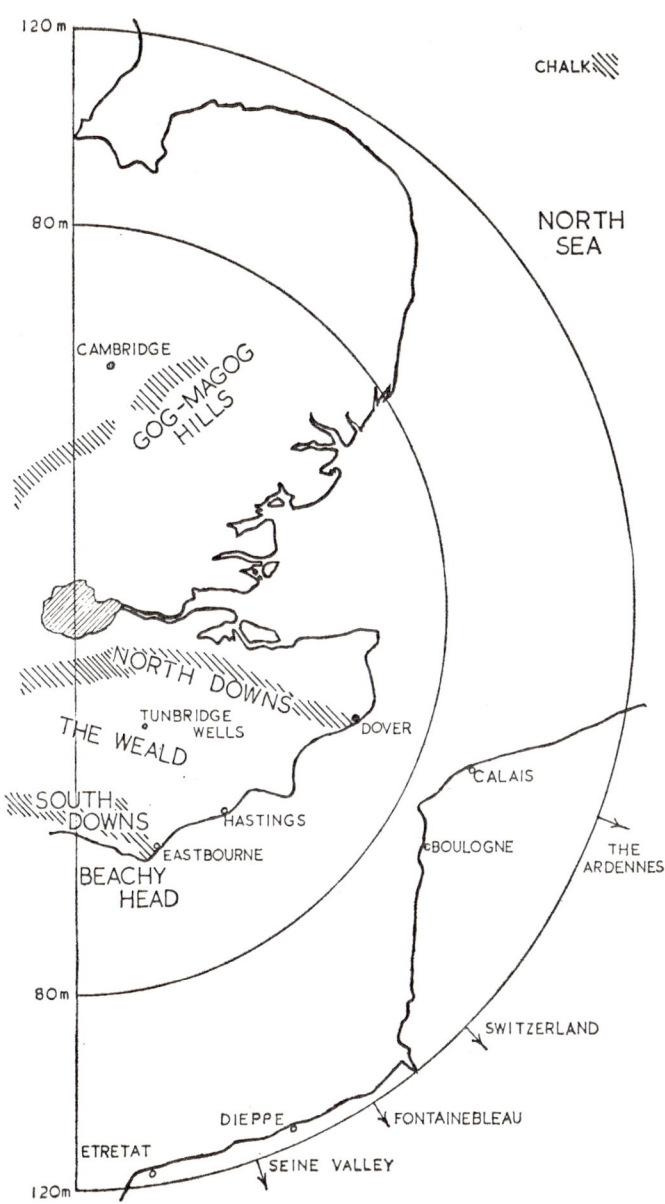

120 m

CHALK

80 m

NORTH
SEA

CAMBRIDGE

GOG-MAGOG
HILLS

NORTH DOWNS

TUNBRIDGE
WELLS

THE WEALD

DOVER

CALAIS

SOUTH
DOWNS

HASTINGS

EASTBOURNE

BOULOGNE

THE
ARDENNES

BEACHY
HEAD

80 m

SWITZERLAND

DIEPPE

FONTAINEBLEAU

ETRETAT

SEINE VALLEY

120m

Sketch plan centred on London—eastern sector

before now supplied a difficult rock chimney; a well-known climber has been seen through a telescope solemnly kicking steps up a steep clay-bank under an overhanging grassy cornice; while a little practice with a woodman's axe or even a blacksmith's hammer may lead the way to the use of the ice-axe.

The answer today follows much the same pattern. First, and most important, comes rock climbing practice essential for keeping climbing muscles in trim and for maintaining a continuous confidence in the approach to rock problems and their solution in positions of reasonable exposure. A special feature of low rocks is the possibility of tackling climbs safeguarded by a rope from above; the removal of the fear of falling is an excellent aid to pushing up standards of performance and sooner or later of leading ability. If there are pinnacles or isolated rock masses only accessible to the rock climber another very basic mountaineering urge can be fulfilled in their ascent. In a countryside completely lacking in exposures of living rock it is appropriate to notice other features which the climber may sometimes use—quarries, where the rock quality improves with age, trees, haystacks, bridges, buildings, and so on. None is so varied or so worthwhile as natural rock, though quarries indeed have played a small part in climbing history.

Second, we come to walking, still the most used activity in all mountaineering wherever it is done. We walk for preference on hill ridges, with wide valley views, ideally with steep slopes on either hand to define a route along the top for us. The climber can make a gentle progress beguiling the way with a study of local flowers and plants, the birds, the antiquities, the valleys between or perhaps just the vast sweep of the clouds across the sky. The antiquarian-minded is particularly fortunate in that the lines of prehistoric trackways are precisely those which he himself is using, while barrows and hill forts are splendidly sited all around in the high places. On the other hand walks can be turned into fiercely competitive exercises—racing against the clock, taking all hills by their steepest ways, boosting uphill and racing down again with bone-jarring haste. The climber can make long-distance marathon walks from point to point, or link together a series of hill tops or a series of features of the same type, in expeditions which demand considerable endurance even if not particularly difficult in detail. It is important however to remember in this sort of situation that all these activities are meant to give pleasure; when training for the sake of training takes over, the individual may develop his muscles but he loses much of the mental stimulus of the more leisurely pursuits. The new sport of orienteering, in which the participants find their way with map and compass from point to point over a course in rough country, is a fine prospect for the ardent walker. It does not involve racing, but rather requires an intelligent eye for the country both on the map and in the field.

The third possible activity for the local climber is coasteering, which I have defined elsewhere as the application of the principles of mountaineering to the features of the coastline. The coasteer walks along cliff tops and beaches, he does conventional rock climbing on sea cliffs as well as traversing along the shore between high and low water marks, he ascends pinnacles and stacks on the foreshore and off-shore, he explores sea caves, using a boat or a rope ladder when necessary to supplement the normal equipment of the rock climber.

In this book I shall demonstrate how these various facilities are made available in the countryside of south-east England for the large numbers of climbers who need them. Here more than anywhere else in the country it is important to emphasise that the mention of a crag, cliff, cave, hill walk or shore does not necessarily imply a right to climb or to enter. There is very little wild open country and almost everywhere is in fact private property, even if it does not appear to be particularly cared for. Entry may be by usage or on sufferance, less frequently by right. In these cultivated and inhabited counties good relations with the local people are especially vital and the traveller, whatever his purpose in the countryside, must behave in a careful and responsible manner.

All sites mentioned in the text can be located by means of the Ordnance Survey National Grid Reference given for each one in the Index. The co-ordinate system can be easily understood by reference to any One Inch Ordnance Survey map.

Though there have been changes for the worse during the last thirty years, there are still many parts of south-east England which are unspoilt. They may stay so for our children and even for our grandchildren, but anyone picking up this book a hundred years from now may well find it a quaint historical record of things long past. When the preservation of scenery rested in the hands of private landowners, their self-interest resisted change and everyone benefitted. The state however is incapable of sustaining preservation movements. National Parks, marvellous in concept, do not work; they are just not permitted to preserve landscape and every interest —military, industrial, hydro-electric etc—invariably prevails against them; finally when legal powers are used to deprive the National Trust the preservation movement will be in a sad state indeed. If we wish to save this countryside of ours it behoves everyone of us to fight and keep on fighting. Let us go out now and take a look at it.

1

NORTH DOWNS AND GREENSANDS

THE Weald of south-east England is a well-defined geological area, the geomorphology of which has been broadly understood since the early years of the nineteenth century. In Cretaceous times, that is between 60 and 120 million years ago, a succession of strata—sandstones, clays and chalks—was laid down in this area, some when it was at the bottom of the sea, others when it was submerged by a great fresh-water lake. The oldest of these rocks, relevant to present-day scenery, was the Wealden Sandstone, then came the Weald Clay, followed by Lower Greensand, Gault Clay, Upper Greensand and finally Chalk. This massive series of beds, having a total thickness of nearly 4,000 ft, was elevated into an elongated dome during the great earth movements associated with the building of the Alps. The axis of the dome ran through south-eastern England, across where the English Channel now lies, and on into France. The rivers which drained the dome ran north and south off it, thus initiating the drainage pattern here which seems such a strange feature in present-day topography. In succeeding ages this dome was progressively eroded, exposing the most recent strata, the chalk, round the edges and the others successively in parallel concentric outcrops to the oldest, the Wealden Sandstone, along the original axis. At some stage, too, the sea broke through along the line of the English Channel, exposing the ends of all the various strata one after the other along the coast. That the lowest beds of this series outcrop at the surface nowadays in the central Weald at a height of 500 to 900 ft gives some idea of the tremendous scale of the erosion that has taken place—in fact 2,500 to 3,000 ft. The ringing hills of chalk and of Lower Greensand all have their scarp slopes facing towards the centre of the dome, with gentler dip slopes running away from it on the other. As the central dome diminished, the rivers cutting ever downwards, still on their original lines, made at intervals in the rim of chalk hills those gaps which are such a distinctive feature of the scenery today.

Starting in the neighbourhood of Dover and the South Foreland, the North Downs run for some 90 miles to Farnham in west Surrey. The only substantial change of general direction, from west-north-west to west-south-west, takes place close to the Medway Gap. The highest point of the North Downs, 882 ft, is near Botley Hill at the top of Titsey Hill in east Surrey. Two miles further east Betsom's Hill (824 ft) above Westerham is the county summit of Kent; the county summit of Surrey, however, is not on the chalk but on the parallel ridge of Lower Greensand. The whole length of the North Downs is traversed by an ancient trackway, the Harroway, which was the main route from the Salisbury Plain area, centre of pre-historic England, to the short crossing to the Continent. The antiquity of the way is unknown, it certainly dates back to the Iron Age and is probably much older. There are alternative routes in a number of places. The crest line of the hills is sometimes over-grown with trees which flourish on the newer deposits of clay-with-flints lying on the top of the chalk, so that the way often followed the comparatively dry base of the chalk just above the heavy clays of the valley, sufficiently high at the same time to enable travellers to see out over the country. This line, moreover, provided short cuts where the crest line would have involved de-tours round embayments in the scarp. The Harroway was used in medieval times by pilgrims travelling to the shrine at Canter-bury from Winchester or who joined the route somewhere along the way. When spring came, as Chaucer tells us:

> Than longen folk to goon on pilgrimages
> To ferne halwes, couthe in sondry londes;
> And specially, from every shires ende
> Of Engelond, to Caunterbury they wende,
> The holy blisful martir for to seke,
> That hem hath holpen, whan that they were seke.

There is little doubt that the pilgrims sometimes made detours to visit religious houses and sites *en route*. For example they would probably have crossed the River Wey at Guildford close to the sandstone hills where the churches of St Catherine and St Martha could be visited. In many places the name 'Pilgrims' Way' is still used to designate parts of this ancient route. The pilgrims left the Harroway when they turned aside to Canterbury through the Stour

Gap, yet on towards Folkestone we still find 'Pilgrims' Way' marked on the Ordnance Survey map on the line of the more ancient way, the one probably used by pilgrims from the Continent. Hilaire Belloc has written a charming book about it—*The Old Road*. The North Downs are not such a well-defined topographical feature as the South Downs, lacking the obvious continuity and compactness of the latter. Particularly in Surrey they have been built over, the suburbs of London creeping slowly up the dip slopes and the isolated houses of those able to live even further afield cropping up on vantage points with views over the Weald. In places the distant views are cut off by the parallel ridge of the Lower Greensand, but the so-called Vale of Holmesdale on the clays between the two becomes then much more striking. The North Downs do not lend themselves to obvious long-distance walks and indeed I have not heard of anyone who has walked them from end to end in one expedition. However, small sections are very suitable for day walks for Londoners and these hills are used extensively for this purpose. Many a budding mountaineer at an early age has seen his first view from a hilltop at just such a place as Colley Hill, Box Hill or Newlands Corner. One looks down, with the eye of a bird, on an inhabited and very English landscape. There are roads threaded by tiny cars, railways traced out by toy trains, church spires and towers, fields and woods, the glint of the sun on some distant window—the young onlooker feels, perhaps for the first time, that though the world seems very large it is in fact a large collection of familiar things. Some days the view shades off mysteriously into thick haze—what lies beyond only dimly seen? Sometimes it is so clear you can reach out and seemingly almost touch a distant object with the finger; sometimes when rods of rain sweep across the hillsides it is a grim, almost alien world fierce and forbidding; sometimes on a bright day of summer the flowers glow, the birds sing and all is light, while if it snows at the other end of the year, then these are mountains indeed.

* * *

Behind the Warren at Folkestone the first hills of the North Downs rise to nearly 600 ft. The scarp line facing south runs inland behind the town by Sugarloaf Hill, Caesar's Camp and the earthworks on Castle Hill. There is a fine view over the Folkestone coastline; the shores of France can often be seen and Fairlight Down beyond Romney Marsh. Almost immediately the magic words 'Pilgrims' Way' appear on the Ordnance Survey map; any pilgrims hereabouts must have been coming from the Continent. After a mile or two the outliers of Summerhouse Hill and Tolsford Hill rise in front of the scarp. The Pilgrims' Way continues mostly on minor roads to Wye in the Stour Gap. In this part of the Downs the chalk covers a wide area to the south of the River Stour, which from the gap at Wye flows through Canterbury, then eastwards to the sea at Pegwell Bay. Beyond the river the chalk outcrops again, forming the Isle of Thanet, where it is exposed extensively in sea cliffs. The Kentish coalfield is in the hinterland behind Deal, while at Eastry there is an extensive chalk cave system, no longer accessible and its original purpose no longer obvious.

For over 20 miles, between the Stour and the Medway gaps, the Pilgrims' Way conducts us west-north-westerly along the foot of the scarp by pathway, track and minor road. Belloc says of it:

> This section might indeed be taken as a type of what the primitive wayfarers intended when the conditions offered them for their journey were such as they would have chosen out of all. . . . The road goes parallel to and above the line where the sharp spring of the hill leaves the floor of the valley; it commands a sufficient view of what is below and of what lies before; it is well on the chalk, just too high to interfere with cultivation, at least with the cultivation of those lower levels to which the Middle Ages confined themselves; it is well dried by an exposure only a little west of south; it is well drained by the slope and by the porous soil; it is uninterrupted by combes, or any jutting promontories, for the range of hills is here exactly even. In a word, it here possesses every character which may be regarded as normal to the original traveller from the west of England to the Straits of Dover.

The hilltops above reach almost everywhere to 600–650 ft. Celia Fiennes crossed this range at Boxley:

> . . . about 10 miles short of Maidstone you ascend a very steep hill which discovers the whole Country at one view forty mile off backward from whence we came, and a few paces on the top of the hill the descent of the hill on that other side is so great a fall that gives you as full a discovery of the Country all forward, both of which show the variety of grounds intermixt with each other and lesser hills and plaines and rivers which such advanced

grounds present the traveller at one view; this is called Boxlye Hill and is part of the same Ridge of hills which runs along by Epsome.

It is hardly so pastoral nowadays.

In the neighbourhood of the Medway gap is a notable archaeological site with Kit's Coty House, the remains of a Neolithic long barrow, as well as other prehistoric and Roman remains. Belloc devotes considerable space to a discussion of where the Pilgrims' Way crossed the river, coming down in the end in favour of Snodland. Our route climbs back to the foot of the scarp and runs on westwards towards Otford and the gap of the Darent. The Coldrum Stones by Trottiscliffe are another notable antiquity; a mile or two further on A20 climbs up over the scarp at Wrotham Hill. Hereabouts the hills reach 700 ft for the first time. Six miles beyond the Darent and half a mile short of the Kent/Surrey border is Betsom's Hill, the county summit of Kent.

The dip slope here is the principal site of the mysterious deneholes about which so much controversy has raged. These are vertical shafts up to 80 ft deep which penetrate the overlying sands into the chalk strata; sometimes there are footholds on the walls, sometimes regular chambers at the foot, and so on. Numerous explanations of their origins have been advanced; none is completely satisfactory. Harry Pearman in his recent book *Dene-holes* summarises the possibilities as follows—underground silos, hiding places from the Danes (ie Danes holes), flint mines, gold mines, underground dwellings, places of worship, naturally occurring, ice-houses, oubliettes, wells or chalk mines. Apart from the gold mine theory, which is completely fantastic, all are plausible; yet each, except for the chalk mine theory, has also some fairly substantial objection. There is no doubt at all that some dene-holes served as chalk mines, for Pearman quotes at length from *A Synopsis of Husbandry* by Thomas Bannister of Horton Kirby, published at the end of the eighteenth century, which gives a precise account of the digging of such holes for this very purpose. However, continues Pearman, many of the holes were in existence long before this, for as early as 1570 William Lambarde, writing of certain holes near Crayford, said:

> . . . many beasts have tumbled into some of these; it happened a late Noble person, following his Hawke, not without great peril of his life, to fall into one of them, that was at least twelve fathoms deep.

It is impossible to account satisfactorily for the large numbers of dene-holes found in some places within a very small area, for example at Cavey's Spring Wood and Stankeys Wood near Bexley-heath and at Hangman's Wood across the Thames at Grays in Essex. In situations like this, where the separation is small, the chambers at the foot of one hole seldom break through into those of surrounding holes. This seems to defy explanation. The extensive breaks-through at Hangman's Wood were the work of the Essex Field Club in 1884 and are not part of the original. Did excavation cease as soon as it became difficult to swing the container with the dug material straight to the foot of the vertical shaft? Was it cheaper to dig another shaft than to transport material below ground? We shall probably never know the answers.

From time to time unwary or unsuspecting people fall into dene-holes, covered over by time and suddenly revealed by subsidence or otherwise. However, it was not until the turn of the century that cavers began to take an interest. The indefatigable Ernest Baker after moving to London led one or two expeditions to the major dene-hole areas. Among other things he organised a public trip down a hole at Abbey Wood:

> A rough platform was laid over one of the holes, a tripod was erected, with pulley and cradle; everything was provided to ensure comfort and safety; and the lord of the manor, who had taken part in our exploration at Bexley, put up a marquee and provided refreshments for these devotees of science. It was a great field-day when they arrived. Fifty or sixty persons must have gone down in successive parties, and one of us stayed below to receive them and act as cicerone. No end of flashlight photographs were taken; the smoke of these and of the illuminants must have made it very difficult to see anything in the chambers below. At any rate, the shaft soon began to smoke like a vent from a volcano. I stood at the top superintending the tackle, and I noticed a particularly dense column of smoke pouring up in front of one of the ascending passengers. It was a young lady in a picture hat, which article had nearly filled the hole and acted like a piston. The neighbouring hole was descended by means of a couple of builders' ladders, but this was by no means so popular as the cradle.

Subsequently there have been many temporary enthusiasts who have played at dene-holes at some time in their caving careers. My own share is perhaps typical. Just after the end of the war a party of climbers descended one of the shafts in Hangman's Wood. We went on to explore, during the lunch-hour, our own local hole behind the gas-works at St Mary Cray and someone else's in a field by Knockholt. Since then I have never looked at another.

It was left to Harry Pearman of the Chelsea Speleological Society to make a systematic approach. By painstaking research into old books and records, by letters to the press and local enquiry he produced in 1966 the book to which we have already referred and which is for the present the 'last word' on the subject. The dene-hole sites extend from the coast by Dover along the North Downs to reach their greatest density in the Bexleyheath area, after which they thin out as we go on westwards.

Away down the dip slope also are the extensive former chalk mines at Chislehurst. These are open to the public as show caves with conducted tours; claims of incredible antiquity have often been made for them. The matter was really settled in the correspondence columns of the *Times* during 1937, triggered by an account in the newspaper of a descent into some old mine workings at St Mary Cray, where there was, it said, 'no indication that they have been entered since Roman times, when the Druids were driven out'. They were connected, the claim went on, with Chislehurst Caves where there were 'thirty miles of explored passages hewn out of the chalk with deer antlers, the marks clearly visible'. Next, an anthropoligst, Sir Arthur Keith, wrote accusing archaeologists of neglecting the caves of north Kent: 'the evidence of prehistoric toil at Chislehurst is much greater than that to be seen at Avebury'. The authoritative voice which closed the controversy was that of Arthur Bonner, a noted archaeologist, who had devoted fifteen years to the problems of chalk caves and mines in south-east England. The mines at Chislehurst date, he said, from the eighteenth century with features introduced in 1830 and later. In 1830 they were used as a source of lime and chalk for farmers and for gun-flints. There is no question of great antiquity and the 'deerhorn pick-marks are fanciful'. At a liberal estimate there are 6 miles of passages.

Passing into Surrey beyond Betsom's Hill we soon find the Downs are even higher, reaching 882 ft at Botley Hill above Titsey. In the miles ahead much of the chalk scarp has Upper Greensand outcropping along its base. One of the component beds, known as hearthstone or firestone, has been worked considerably in the past

—to be used long ago as a building stone and later for the floors of hearths or furnaces and for whitening domestic hearths and doorsteps. It was quarried in the open at first, then as time went on, excavated by tunnelling; as most records refer to both processes as quarrying it is difficult to say when one gave way to the other. Many of these tunnels remain today, providing a type of caving for the London enthusiast, not necessarily very much like the real thing, but fascinating nevertheless because of the human associations. All this is recorded in two books published by the Chelsea Speleological Society—*Secret Tunnels in Surrey* by H. Pearman (1963), and *More Secret Tunnels in Surrey* by J. Henderson, B. Hillman and H. Pearman (1968). Little active quarrying seems to have taken place for the last fifty years, though the tunnels have seen recent use for mushroom growing and for the storage of this, that and the other particularly in wartime; sometimes exits get blocked naturally or on purpose, sometimes others appear as a result of digging or subsidence.

The principal series lies close to A22 north of Godstone. There are many miles of fairly uniform passages, blocked in places by roof falls, which interconnect in a bewildering fashion. Others, sometimes open and sometimes closed, are to be found at Betchworth, Colley Hill above Reigate, Merstham and Gatton.

The hearthstone mine at Colley Hill, now permanently sealed, was closed at one time by a very stout door with a gap of roughly 8 in below. Cavers have to be fully alive to the dimensions of gaps through which they can crawl and in those days we took a keen interest in just this problem, even practising at home with obstacle courses of chairs and table legs. Concluding that we could in fact get through this 8 in, a verification expedition was promoted. On the spot a few struggles and kicks saw us all inside, but unfortunately an observant local saw us also and fearing the worst, telephoned the police. After an interesting and intensive circuit of the workings, the struggles and kicks below the door were reversed directly into the hands of the local force. We were marched off to interview the owner; the decline of my interest in London caving dates from the ensuing time of awkward explanations. One should of course go about it in a different way and seek prior permission for attempts of this type, if indeed they are worth bothering about at all. Apart from the hearthstone mines a whole range of curiosities in the category of caves are listed in the works mentioned above. These, which might repay the odd explorer who has obtained previous permission, include secret passages and tunnels, wells and conduits, air-raid shelters and military works dug in hillsides, ice-houses and various sorts of follies.

The Pilgrims' Way leads on westwards with the usual mixture of footpath, cart-track and minor road, broken here and there by sections on private land which have to be circumvented. Way down the dip slope is a quarry worthy of note because it was mentioned by the author of *Rock Climbs round London*—'a good but rather public quarry half a mile from Warlingham Station on the right going north'—from which we have to infer, though he does not say so, that he had climbed there. It can be viewed from the trains, passing on their way to the rocks at Groombridge; we were never attracted in the slightest, though it was occasionally suggested that a spray of liquid concrete would improve the prospects. Geoffrey Winthrop Young has called chalk climbing 'the missing link between rock and ice technique', but one would hardly wish to verify his theories in surroundings as public as these.

A popular section of the Downs is that above Reigate, where Reigate and Colley Hills are just below 800 ft. So steep and so embayed is the scarp that the Pilgrims' Way for a time runs along the top of the ridge, crossing the Brighton road (A23) by a suspension bridge. 'Surely', says Belloc, 'the only example in Europe of so modern an invention serving to protect the record of so remote a past.' Beyond Pebblecombe the route drops down again to its familiar position below the scarp passing below the huge chalk pits at Betchworth. Chalk was obtained for agricultural purposes from great open quarries such as these; there are tunnelled workings also. The white scars on the green of the hillsides can be seen for many a mile, so that for Belloc they were 'the chief landmarks of the county':

> I looked up at their immensity and considered how often I had seen them through the haze; two patches of white shining over the Weald to where I might be lying on the crest of my own Downs, thirty miles away.

Below these quarries at Betchworth, say Harper and Kershaw, 200 tons of hearthstone a week were produced at one time, providing employment for as many as fifty men, 'real old Surrey rustics':

The quarry entrance is just a small hole in the hillside, like the workings for a small tunnel, not like a mine shaft. This unimpressive entrance, however, rather astonishingly branches out, when once you enter, in all directions, for the workings have in the course of years become very extensive. They are by no means lofty; and, indeed, a tall man can scarce stand upright in them. It is cold and dank and damp within, and work is carried on by means of oil lanterns and candles. Horses are employed in pulling out the trolley-loads of stone, and are provided with great soft pads fixed to their heads, in case they throw them up into violent contact with the roof, which is liberally propped with timbers.

This was in 1923; there is no longer any access to the extensive system of passages they describe.

Soon we come to Box Hill above the Dorking Gap, only 563 ft yet surely the best-known hill in the South East. Slopes clad with the trees from which it gets its name, 'it stands out', notes Belloc, 'like a cape along our coasting journey, the strongest and most simple of our southern hills'. There is a road to the summit and an indicator; the slopes above the gap are steep, those running north towards Burford Bridge being highly suitable for ski-ing when conditions are right. There is heathland to the north and east— Walton Heath, Hedley Heath, Epsom Downs etc—very popular day-walking country.

By way of the Dorking Gap the River Mole breaks through the Downs from its source in the Weald to join the Thames at Molesey. This river is of special interest to cavers because just beyond Box Hill it disappears, in whole or in part, into a series of swallet holes and, flowing for a time underground, reappears at springs near Leatherhead. The interesting possibility is that there might be a cave system of sorts here similar to a series of natural caves discovered by waterworks men at Strood in Kent and to others found recently in chalk strata in France. No one has yet entered the system, nor has any serious attempt been made to dig into it. The early topographical writers all commented on this curious phenomenon. Michael Drayton, for example:

> Mole digs herself a path by working day and night,
> According to her name to show her nature right,
> And underneath the earth for three miles space doth creep,
> Till gotten out of sight quite from her mother's keep.

Celia Fiennes referred to Camden's story of a duck:

. . . forced into one of the holes, which came out at the other side by Molesey with its feathers almost all rubbed off.

Her comment applies equally to all the variants of this popular story, which crops up in various forms all over the country:

. . . how they could force the Duck into so difficult a way or whether anything of this is more than Conjecture must be left to everyone's liberty to judge.

The line of the Downs continues through famous walking country by Ranmore Common, Hackhurst Downs and Netley Heath to Newlands Corner, a notable viewpoint accessible to the motor car. For part of this section the Lower Greensand ridge only a few miles to the south overtops the chalk and blocks the view across the Weald. The narrow strip of Gault Clay crowded between these ridges, known as the Vale of Holmesdale, is an outstanding feature of the landscape. The Downs now drop abruptly to the Wey Gap which is blocked by the City of Guildford. There are some fragments of a medieval castle with nearby an extensive cave system almost certainly a mine for building stone; unfortunately the entrance has recently had to be blocked up. The Pilgrims' Way, still on the south face of the hills, descended by St Martha's and the Chantries and crossed the Wey by ferry to St Catherine's on the west bank. This hill, says Defoe:

. . . on top of the ascent from the town carries the gallows, which is so placed, respecting the town, that the townspeople from the High Street may sit at their shop doors, and see the criminals executed.

Stretching on westwards is the Hog's Back, a continuation of the chalk ridge having the dip now much steeper so that the flanking slopes to the north and south give comparable views across wide plains. Defoe passing this way noted:

. . . the ridge of a high chalky hill, so narrow that the breadth of the road takes up the breadth of the hill, and the declivity begins on either hand, at the very hedge that bounds the highway, and is very steep, as well as very high; from this hill is a prospect either way, so far that it is surprising; and one sees to the north, or northwest, over the great black desert, called Bagshot Heath one way, and the other way south-east into Sussex, almost to the South Downs, and west to an unbounded length. . . .

The once wild heathlands of Bagshot Heath and Cobham Common have suffered severely from military occupation. We no longer find as Defoe did:

> . . . a vast tract of land, some of it within 17 or 18 miles of the capital city, which is horrid and frightful to look on, not only good for little, but good for nothing; much of it a sandy desert, and one may frequently be put in mind of Arabia Deserta.

How marvellous if it were still like that today! There is indeed plenty of rough and unkept country about but we are never very far from one or other of the more morbid accompaniments of modern living.

On northward between these heaths and the Thames is the Great Park at Windsor and a minor climbing site. In *Wall and Roof Climbing* (1905), Geoffrey Winthrop Young described the Copper Horse in the Park as 'an excellent elementary problem'. Years later H. Courtney Bryson took up the challenge:

> The pudding-like statue of George the Third in Windsor Great Park is supported by a rocky granite plinth which provides several good climbs (boots or rubbers) and a girdle traverse. A study of the Rules and Regulations relating to Windsor Great Park shows that, while it is prohibited to climb trees and fences, no mention is made of the plinths of statues. Though a plinth is not a wall within the meaning of the Act, a preliminary reconnaissance is advisable.

Farnham marks the end of the Hog's Back. The Pilgrims' Way, as described by Hilaire Belloc, runs on up the valley of the Wey, crosses the chalk by a pass of nearly 700 ft into the valley of the Itchen and so down to Winchester, the route in these days almost entirely on made-up roads. The more ancient Harroway pressed on westwards by lines now largely lost to us to join the trackways on the downs beyond Basingstoke.

*   *   *

Parallel to the chalk and nearer the centre of the dome is an outcropping ridge of Lower Greensand. Though lacking the continuity of the chalk over long distances, this forms many upstanding hills which are often higher and which have scarp slopes facing similarly towards the centre of the Weald. The oldest rocks in the area, the Wealden Sands, which we shall deal with later, form a hill block at the core of the Weald. All these various strata, after dipping beneath the London Basin, reappear to the north; the chalk, as we shall see, forms the Chiltern Hills, while the Lower Greensand and the Wealden Sands also make an appearance.

The Lower Greensand, which comprises in places various strata of limestone and clay as well as a variety of sands seldom green, forms low cliffs at Sandgate west of Folkestone. For the first 25 miles the hills are not especially high, reaching only 200–300 ft. Between Leeds Castle and Hollingbourne there used to be a complex man-made cave system from which sand was obtained for glass making. The glass for the Great Exhibition of 1851, which later became Crystal Palace, came from here. The well-known speleologist Ernest Baker and the archaeologist Professor Bonner were once lost in these tunnels. As Baker recorded it:

> To go on with the survey in the time we had was obviously futile; all we could achieve was a superficial exploration, and we must be on the look-out not to lose ourselves in the ramifications. But with little delay we found this was exactly what we had done. For an hour or more we marched hither and thither along the twisting passages, our backs bent double beneath the low roof, vainly trying to locate ourselves by the compass. The passages were so much alike we were not sure of recognising any given spot if we came back to it. At last we adopted the final resource in such a quandary—to bear steadily in one direction, the right or the left, follow every turning to the end, and, retracing our steps, repeat the manœuvre. By this process of elimination, although it was complicated by the presence of an upper as well as a lower series, we at length found our way back to the mushrooms. It was long after dark, and when with aching back-bones we reached the inn again, the dinner we had gaily ordered on arrival was a midnight supper.

These tunnels have recently been entirely destroyed by road makers. Further on in Senacre Wood near Broughton, 2 miles south of Maidstone, is a small cave in the Kentish Rag, a local limestone once used as a building stone, as it was, for example, in the original Roman Wall of London. Near Loose one of the local streams flows for some distance underground and this may well indicate some sort of natural cave in this same limestone.

Beyond Maidstone the sandstone hills begin to take on stature. They reach 550 ft in the extensive Mereworth Woods and further on 660 ft in the neighbourhood of Ightham. On Oldbury Hill there are Palaeolithic rock shelters, also an Iron Age fort. The small rock exposures hereabouts are unfortunately not high enough for the adult climber. It was Courtney Bryson who first drew attention to some monoliths at Park Place beside the Sevenoaks to Tonbridge road, but I have never met anyone who has seen them. At Ide Hill and Toys Hill, south of Westerham, these hills of Lower Greensand at last reach a height comparable with that of the parallel chalk ridge; Toys Hill is 801 ft while Betsom's Hill on the chalk, $3\frac{1}{2}$ miles to the north west, only overtops it by 23 ft. On Hosey Common beside the road from Westerham to Crockham Hill there is another small cave in the sand. Approaching Redhill the ridge is lower and contains big deposits of Fuller's Earth, which are extensively worked. At Reigate there is a show cave in the sandstone in the centre of the town beneath the old castle mound.

Beyond the Dorking Gap the Lower Greensand reaches its greatest elevation in the trinity of Leith, Holmbury and Pitch Hills; beds of chert in the sandstone produce a fine escarpment all along the south flank and there are splendid views out over the Weald. Leith Hill (965 ft), the highest hill south of London, was the scene of a great battle in AD 851 between the Danes and the West Saxons. A tower on the summit, built to its present height in 1864, reaches to 1,000 ft above sea level; an indicator on the battlements enables many distant landmarks to be identified. A hundred years ago a group of mountaineers, calling themselves the Sunday Tramps, used to walk on these hills under the leadership of Leslie Stephen, the noted Alpinist:

> I can comfort myself now and then, when the fellow-passengers who tread on my heels in London have put me out of temper, by thinking of Leith Hill. It only rises to the height of 1,000 feet by

---

(above) Leith Hill and the Weald. The viewpoint is Pitch Hill; Holmbury Hill lies between; *(below left)* sandstone tunnels at Beddington, typical man-made tunnels of the South East. It is surprising how much of this sort of thing has rewarded the diligent searcher during the last two or three decades; *(below right)* Windsor Great Park. The granite plinth of this statue of George III is said to have been climbed upon

the help of the "Folly" on the top, but you can see, says my authority, twelve counties from the tower; and, if certain legendary Ordnance surveyors spoke the truth, distinguish the English Channel to the south, and Dunstable Hill far beyond the border to the north. The Crystal Palace, too, as we are assured, 'sparkles like a diamond'.

Other viewers have variously reported—forty-one London churches, Beachy Head, the Isle of Wight, steamers and sail in the Channel, and Windsor Castle, but some of these sightings require rare and exceptional visibility.

Next to the west comes Holmbury Hill. Frank Smythe, eminent Himalayan mountaineer and perhaps the leading mountaineering writer of the thirties, describes the view of these hills from the north:

The little church of St Martha's, which stands by the Pilgrims' Way, is a lovely viewpoint. We stood there and looked across the moonlit hills from Hascombe to Holmbury and Leith Hill, and saw between Hascombe and Hurt Wood Hill the level line of the Weald. Bands of diaphanous vapour lying in the valleys picked out the crests of the ridges, which rose, one after the other, in dark orderly waves. And over all reigned an immense peacefulness. Not silence —there is never absolute silence in a countryside—but peace.

Dawn found us on Blackheath Common. There was nothing dramatic in its advent, no fierce and wild rush of colouring, no bold sallies, nothing to ape the drama and pageantry of an Alpine dawn. It was an opening of dim eyes, a gradual realisation of wakefulness. . . . We sat down to rest for a moment. . . .

Four hours later . . . the sun was well up and fast drying the dew, the fresh air was full of bird song, and a light breeze was stirring the gorse and heather. We ate breakfast, then went on our

———

South Downs from Devil's Dyke, looking west along the scarp towards the unmistakable beech clump of Chanctonbury

way and, true to Alpine tradition, ate another and larger breakfast at the first inn we came to.

All that day we lounged along the hills: Hurt Wood Hill, Pitch Hill, Holmbury Hill and Leith Hill. It mattered nothing to us how many miles we covered or the time we took to cover them. We walked when we liked and rested when we liked. There can be few eminences whence the eye can take in more of England's beauty than Holmbury Hill.

This was in the *Spirit of the Hills* in which we find him pressing forward towards a philosophical integration of the whole range of activities which is mountaineering. It stretches from these low hills right up to the Himalaya and embraces the ascents, the views and our reactions to being upon them, be they major or minor. Anyone entering the range does so at a point suited to his opportunities, his inclinations and his abilities; from the broad viewpoint, all are mountaineers.

After Holmbury comes Pitch Hill above Cranleigh, closely followed by Hascombe Hill with its camp 'lying out in the Weald like a Spithead fort', Holloways Heath and the curiously named Hydon's Ball (formerly Highdown Ball). These are substantially wooded but there are often fine views towards Hindhead and Black Down. Some climbing has been done on the Bargatestone Beds of the Lower Greensand in a quarry near Godalming. Originally explored by Wilfrid Noyce and used by boys from Charterhouse, this is no longer accessible. Beyond to the west lies an extensive area of sandy heathland—the Commons of Ockley, Thursley, Hankley, Frensham, and so on. These extend to the neighbourhood of Farnham where Crooksbury Hill, 'lifting like a dark pyramid', closes the view. Beyond it the heathland continues northwards, unattractive now because of the military occupation of Aldershot, Farnborough and the rest.

2

THE SOUTH DOWNS
AND NEIGHBOURING HILLS

FROM Farnham the chalk wall of the Weald pivots round the heaths and hills of the Lower Greensand for about 18 miles, forming the edge of a block of chalk country which stretches westwards for many miles to Salisbury Plain. Past Selborne, made famous by Gilbert White, is Butser Hill (888 ft), the start and also the highest point of the South Downs. This is Hampshire, but it is not the county summit, which is in fact Pilot Hill in the far north. The highest point of the South Downs in Sussex is Tegleaze Down (836 ft), near Up-Waltham; this too is not the county summit which is Black Down on the Lower Greensand.

From Butser Hill the South Downs run due east for almost 60 miles until cut off by the sea in great cliffs between Brighton and Eastbourne. Recently designated an 'Area of Outstanding Natural Beauty' by the Countryside Commission, this ridge is much more distinctive than its northern counterpart, which faces it across the Weald. Here too a prehistoric trackway follows the ridge, keeping this time mostly on the top edge of the scarp. There are abundant relics of early man. The traverse from end to end is an obvious hill walk of some considerable merit, which members of the Society of Sussex Downsmen carry out every Easter taking four days over it. Smaller sections delineated by the river gaps serve for day walks which are no less worthy. The views from these hills embrace not only the broad miles of the Weald to the north, here never obscured by overtopping ridges of Lower Greensand, but also on the other side, the Channel coast which draws ever nearer as we move eastwards.

Gilbert White has been scorned for calling the Downs 'that chain of majestic mountains'. True their height is only that of hills (mountains, say his critics, are built on a larger scale altogether), yet majestic they certainly are and they have many of the attributes of mountains—continuity, a striking outline and a bold uplift above the plains, like a great green wave rolling up the Wealden strand, far seen and far seeing. Mountains, we feel, should be sharp pointed, rocky and abrupt; the South Downs are none of these but rounded, smooth and flowing. Gilbert White appreciated just this about them, saying:

> I think there is somewhat peculiarly sweet and amusing in the shapely-figured aspect of the chalk hills in preference to those of stone, which are rugged, broken, abrupt and shapeless.

*   *   *

We take up once again our walk along the edge of the chalk.

From Farnham the chalk ridge continues along the north edge of the Wey valley reaching 738 ft, 2 miles from Alton. South of the valley the villages of Binstead and Selborne stand on a platform of Upper Greensand, the firestone or hearthstone strata already mentioned as being mined in Surrey. West of this sandstone strip there is a scarp edge of the Hampshire chalk block. Selborne is famous as the home of Gilbert White, the outstanding eighteenth-century naturalist; his *Natural History of Selborne*, consisting of a long series of letters to Thomas Pennant and Daines Barrington, contains a host of observations of nature, set forth in a simple and direct language which is a joy to read. Even today pleasant walking can be found hereabouts and we can still recognise something of the countryside that White knew so well:

> The high part to the south-west consists of a vast hill of chalk, rising 300 feet above the village; and is divided into a sheep down, the high wood and a long hanging wood called the Hanger. The covert of this eminence is altogether beech, the most lovely of forest trees. . . . The down, or sheep walk, is a pleasing park-like spot, of about one mile by half that space jutting out on the verge of the hill country, where it begins to break down into the plains, and commanding a very engaging view, being an assemblage of hill, dale, woodlands, heath and water. . . . At the foot of this hill, one stage or one step from the uplands, lies the village, which consists of a single straggling street, ¾ mile in length, in a sheltered vale, and running parallel with the Hanger.

Noar Hill (695 ft) to the south, White tells us, lies on the watershed between the English Channel and the North Sea, feeding water to the former by the Arun and to the latter by the Wey and the Thames. There are others of the hillside beech woods known as

Hangers. That at Hawkley was the scene of a great landslide in March 1774:

> a considerable part of the great woody hanger at Hawkley was torn from its place and fell down, leaving a high freestone cliff naked and bare, and resembling the steep side of a chalk pit.

Two houses and a barn were destroyed, but no one was killed. Some fifty years later William Cobbett, passing on one of his Rural Rides, makes no mention of this, but impressed he certainly was by the view:

> . . . it was like looking from the top of a castle down into the sea, except that the valley was land not water.

Now only 5 miles away to the south is Butser Hill, the start and the highest point of the South Downs.

Butser Hill (888 ft) was once a monarch among hills, as Massingham tells us:

> No fewer than eight spurs with almost headlong combes between them taper down from the circular plateau and make it the star-fish of the southern hills. The flanks of these combes are, most of them, mantled in trees, and the south-eastern spur in a yew forest most venerable, with silver-flashing whitebeam and the green turf about it to darken its shades yet deeper. But the grey-green plateau itself is bare, except for patches of primeval scrub-bowed and knotted thorn, huddled furze and juniper stiffly formal in design and yet the wildest of all the wild growths in England.

Now with a motor road almost to the summit and crowned with radio masts it has lost completely its royal stature. We leave it therefore as quickly as possible and set out on our trek eastwards. Almost immediately we have to cross the busy Portsmouth road, once in a deep cutting, but now claiming more and more of the hill as widening and double tracking scar the slopes. Soon the hurrying motor traveller will hardly be aware that he is crossing a hill range at all. Beyond is quiet; less than a mile ahead below the north face of the ridge is Buriton, the start of a modern long-distance bridle path and walking route, the Countryside Commission's South Downs Ridgeway. This follows the ancient trackways over the hilltops to the sea at Eastbourne some 60 miles away. We follow it and soon cross the county border into Sussex. The first long section of the Downs, running for some 25 miles from

Butser Hill to the Arun Gap is more wooded than the part further east; in places there are beech woods on both scarp and dip slopes.

Down below at Harting terminated the spendid cross-country walk described by Belloc in *Four Men*, which, S. P. B. Mais tells us, is still followed sometimes by his fans. The book tells of a tuneful and philosophical journey from inn to inn by four highly assorted companions, starting at Robertsbridge far away in East Sussex and walking, in the course of five days, along the sandstone hills to Lower Beeding by Horsham, south across the Weald clays to Steyning, then along the foot of the Downs here to Harting. This would also be a suitable expedition for a modern walker.

Beacon Hill above Treyford, with a rectangular hill fort, was the site during the Napoleonic wars of a semaphore used to relay messages from Portsmouth towards London. Nearby on the south side of Treyford Hill are the Devil's Jumps, a line of five Bronze Age bell barrows. Next comes Linch Down (813 ft), the second highest point of the Sussex Downs. There is a magnificent view over to Black Down, with Leith Hill and a white gleam from the pits of the North Downs in the distance; to the south are dense forests at first, beyond them the sea, Chichester Harbour and a glimpse of the Isle of Wight. The route descends over Cocking Down to A286.

Down the dip slope to the south of this section, beyond the valley of Chilgrove, is Bow Hill (670 ft)—a notable archaeological site, with four large Bronze Age barrows—the Devil's Humps, the small circular camp of Goosehill, sundry other banks, entrenchments, early field systems and trackways, as well as the site of flint mines.

Between the gap at Cocking and a similar gap south of Duncton, where A285 crosses, there are 5 miles of steep-sided ridge in almost a straight line over Heyshott Down, with a row of eight Bronze Age barrows, Graffham Down and Woolavington Down. There are woods on both scarp and dip. Among the trees half a mile back from the edge is the highest point of the Sussex South Downs, variously called Tegleaze, Littleton Down or Duncton Down (836 ft). The two gap roads converge on Chichester to the south west; in the wedge of Down between them is St Roche's Hill (676 ft) surmounted by the huge circular camp known as the Trundle, actually a Neolithic causewayed camp inside an Iron Age fort.

The view is magnificent—the South Downs from Butser Hill as far as Devil's Dyke, near at hand Goodwood racecourse, the coastal plains towards Chichester and the channel shore. Three miles to the west on the far side of the valley of the Lavant River are the prehistoric sites on Bow Hill already mentioned.

The next section of the main ridge over Barlavington Down, Burton Down and Bignor Hill curves round a large embayment above Bignor village, where there is a noteworthy Roman villa. There are still woods on both flanks of the Downs. At Bignor Hill the Roman Stane Street (Chichester to London) crosses the ridge. The line of the road—substantially straight from Chichester to Pulborough—is well seen from here. For the first 5 miles from Chichester it follows the line of the present A285, but where the latter swerves away to the north to the gap in the ridge by Duncton, Stane Street strikes diagonally up Halnaker Hill, with its windmill, to close on 700 ft and then plunges down the scarp slope past the Roman Villa to Hardham Camp and Pulborough. From our viewpoint on the ridge we can follow the course of the next great alignment from Pulborough to the east shoulder of Leith Hill and beyond that catch a glimpse of the North Downs where Stane Street runs on through the Dorking Gap towards Epsom Downs and London. It is interesting to speculate how the Roman road builders laid out these very considerable straight lines with such precision. Belloc postulates scaffolding erections up to 150 ft high at the ends and large wheeled devices which were moved into line in between. He scorns the possibility of smoke signals, mirrors or lights at night. More recently Winbolt has contended that there would have been no difficulty in making the trace by smoke or other signals, while intermediate points were fixed by a surveying instrument, known as a droma, in which two plummet strings were moved into line with a distant object.

We have now arrived at the deep cleft of the Arun Gap. There is a small castle ruin at Amberley to the north and a fine inhabited castle at Arundel in the south. The next section of the ridge leads on in 7 miles or so to the A24, which crosses a pass of 323 ft between Washington and Findon. This is the beginning of the bare eastern hills; the extensive woodlands are left behind and henceforward we have an almost uninterrupted view down the dip slope to the sea on the one hand and out across the Weald on the other. We feel with Andrew Young:

The surprising thing about these low hills is their height; on their summits you feel yourself nearer to the sky and its cloudy architecture than you do to the Weald. Indeed, walking along their northern escarpment, you feel you are looking down on—the earth.

We come to A24 by Rackham, Kithurst, Sullington and Highden Hills. Southwards on the dip slope are Harrow and Blackpatch Hills, prolific archaeological sites, particularly noteworthy for extensive flint mines. There is also an Iron Age fort.

The short run of hills beyond, between this road and the Adur Gap, is dominated by Chanctonbury Ring (783 ft), one of the best-known of Sussex hills. The ring is a prehistoric earthwork crowning the summit, but the distinguishing feature, which makes the hill outstanding in distant views from all over the Weald, is an isolated clump of beech trees planted 200 years ago over the summit earthwork. Inside the wood it is eerie indeed, contrasting sharply with the wide open face of the downs all round. Three miles to the south Cissbury Ring (602 ft) overlooks Worthing. Here is the largest earthwork in the South Downs occupying some 60 acres; it dates back to the Iron Age and was later used by the Romans. Archaeologists estimate that 35,000 cu yd of chalk were excavated to build the ramparts, the retaining walls for which used around 10,000 15 ft timbers. This scale of construction with the primitive tools available is truly startling. Hereabouts, too, there are sites of Neolithic flint mines.

Where our route crosses the Adur we are only about 3 miles from the sea at Shoreham. The coastline here is considerably built over and its influence spreads with golf courses, radio masts (Truleigh Hill) and electricity pylons (Edburton Hill) up towards the edge of the Downs. The scarp slope is notably steep, so that early geologists were almost persuaded that this was a former cliff line:

> The geologist cannot fail to recognise in this view the exact likeness to a sea cliff, and if he turns and looks in the opposite direction, or eastward, towards Beachy Head, he will see the same line of height prolonged. Even those who are not accustomed to speculate on the former changes which the surface has undergone, may fancy the broad and level plain to resemble the flat sands which were laid dry by the receding tide, and the different projecting masses of Chalk to be the headlands of a coast which separated the different bays from each other.

It was of course never anything of the sort.

The notable scenic attraction is the Devil's Dyke, a deep combe in the north-facing slopes, dug, it is said, by the Devil to let the sea into the Weald. By a misunderstanding he was unable to complete the task during the single night allotted, otherwise this book would be describing substantially different scenery. There is a large camp on the hillside above and an impressive view, which has to be shared with the many pilgrims who come up from Brighton. It is easily possible to walk away from the hotel and the cafés and find comparative solitude along the ridge. Over Newtimber Hill we come to the London–Brighton road (A23) some 6 miles from the Adur.

Even though it is possible to take a car to the summit of Ditchling Beacon, the next section is fine and open. Wolstonbury Hill with its camp and quarries is, in the words of E. V. Lucas:

> . . . the most mountainous of the hills in this part, and indeed, although far from the highest, perhaps the noblest in mien of the whole range, by virtue of its isolation and its conical shape, and, in certain lights, the loveliest.

We pass the windmills, Jack and Jill, on the slopes above Clayton and so on to Ditchling Beacon (813 ft). Now there are two possible routes past Lewes. The first, which is followed by the South Downs Ridgeway, turns south at Plumpton Plain and, after crossing A27, runs over Newmarket and Iford Hills to Rodmell and a crossing of the Ouse at Southease. It is possible however to continue along the main ridge over Mount Harry and down past the battlefield of Lewes into the county town. On the far side the isolated Cliffe Hill and Mount Caburn were the scene in 1836 of a real Alpine-type avalanche, which demolished cottages and killed eight people. Beyond their summits we cross the stream by Glynde, and climb out on to the main ridge again at Beddingham Hill to the south.

My only experience of chalk climbing in a quarry took place over 20 years ago on the south-eastern slopes of Mount Caburn. At first we wore our crampons which, because of World War II, had never been near an ice slope. We were unimpressed when later on we came to try it as rock for climbing, for at that time we were singularly narrow-minded about what was climbable—but we found some fossils and some flowers and saw a fox on a ledge on the face. Later a steep ascent to the earthwork on Caburn was a great delight, and success or failure on the chalk below no longer mattered. I have never been back there.

The next section of the ridge stretches on for 8 miles to the gap of the Cuckmere River. Between the highest hill here, Firle Beacon, and Beddingham Hill, there is a road to the top from West Firle village. Our route continues past the long barrow on Firle Beacon, over Bostal Hill and down to Alfriston village. Here on the slopes of Hindover Hill is the only white horse in Sussex, cut in the turf in 1924 to replace one of 1838 on the same site.

Now there is a block of high ground all the way from the scarp edge to the sea, which cuts off the hills to give a coastline of high cliffs between Eastbourne and Cuckmere Haven. The South Downs Ridgeway climbs Windover Hill from Alfriston, looking down on the carved figure of the Long Man of Wilmington, 230 ft long, which, dating from the Middle Ages, is thought to have been a landmark associated with Wilmington Priory in the valley underneath. To eliminate the need for scouring, the outline was delineated in 1874 with white bricks. Nearby are the barrows—Long Barrow and Hunters' Burgh. The Ridgeway route now makes direct for Eastbourne by Jevington and Willingdon Hill. It would perhaps be more appropriate to follow the scarp edge, now facing east, from Combe Hill above Willingdon village past Eastbourne to Beachy Head, where it ends abruptly at 534 ft, or better still to move southwards parallel to the Cuckmere River and finish along the cliff edge.

We have already written of the Society of Sussex Downsmen and their annual four-day walk of the Ridgeway. This rate of progress is ideal for seeing everything that is by the way and is very much what the day visitor from London will aim for also. The South Downs have, however, a unity which makes the traverse from Butser Hill to Beachy Head the nearest approach in the South East to the long-distance walks in the Peak and the Pennines. There does not seem to be any record of traversing it in one expedition, but there seems no reason to doubt that it could be done, and probably inside twenty-four hours. Some climbers like to pit themselves against this sort of challenge; the hills are there for everyone to enjoy, each in his own way.

*   *   *

For most of the way, looking in towards the centre of the Weald we see the outcrops of the Greensands continuing in a parallel line, sometimes, as in the North Downs, even dominating the ubiquitous chalk.

In the pleasant sandy heath country south of Crooksbury Hill there are several curiosities. Tunnels in the sand have been explored near Farnham (Mother Ludlam's Hole on the banks of the Wey, which goes in for 160 ft), at Puttenham, where a one-time source of glass sand is no longer accessible, and on Thursley Common, a 50 ft passage which may have had some connection with the former iron works. Hankley Common is used apparently for practice parachute jumping; one hot summer's day we toiled up a long sandy slope here and on to a minor hilltop, to be confronted in the hollow beyond with an inflated barrage balloon, tethered close to the ground. No one was in sight. Though familiar to an earlier generation, there cannot be many of them in use nowadays. The Great and Little Ponds at Frensham are inland 'seaside' resorts, very popular with motorists. A short walk southwards takes us soon to three isolated hills set in a row—the Devil's Jumps. 'They hedge the horizon', says Eric Parker, 'like inverted pudding bowls covered with bracken, and with bell heather kindling to crimson in the July sunlight'. The easternmost hill, which belongs to the National Trust, has all the ingredients of a perfect mountain in miniature, well within the powers of the most junior of potential mountaineers. A path up through the woods from the road leads, long before tiredness or boredom have time to set in, to an open heathy hillside surmounted by a small rocky crag some 8 ft high. This can be climbed *en face* by the nimble or circumvented by the youngest—the ground drops away sharply to the north and suddenly there is a tremendous mountain view across miles of heath to Frensham and Crooksbury. The rocks underfoot, says G. M. Davies, are limonite sandstones, 'reputed to be the rusted relics of the thunderbolt hurled by St Michael at the Devil when he was practising at the Jumps'.

South of these splendid little summits the land slopes up to the block of hill country around Hindhead, described by E. C. Matthews in *The Highlands of South West Surrey*:

> The different structure and texture of the rocks have given rise to a bolder form of scenery than is encountered in the Chalk; and in their great elevation, their abruptness of form, and the deep ravines

which furrow their sides, these Southern Highlands more nearly resemble true mountainous country than anything else in this part of England. They stand, an isolated tableland, with a steep escarpment both to north and south, rising into wild hills and high, treeless, heather-clad commons.

Below Gibbet Hill on the northern flanks of the block is the striking combe of the Devil's Punchbowl, with the A3 trunk road climbing up through it. Cobbett's verdict was that 'this is certainly the most villainous spot that God ever made'; G. M. Davies quoting the above in 1939 commented, 'Cobbett had not seen the traffic on the Portsmouth Road'. Both of them should see it now! Gibbet Hill (894 ft), which is in Surrey, is overtopped by Black Down 4 miles away beyond Haslemere. This hill at the south-east corner of the block, remote and tree-covered, is at 919 ft the highest in Sussex and the second highest in this part of England.

Facing Black Down over the village of Fernhurst is the scarp slope of the southern part of the Lower Greensand outcrop which here reaches 676 ft at Telegraph Hill (with the long barrow of Bevis's Thumb), and 625 ft at Bexley Hill, currently threatened with a television mast. Along the dip slopes between here and the scarp of the South Downs flows the River Rother. The ridge runs back eastwards parallel to the chalk, but hereafter the hills are never so substantial as those in the northern Weald. Somewhere by Pulborough there is an extensive cave system in the sandstone, while at Codmore Hill Farm north of the town a small quarry, also sandstone, has been persuaded to yield half a dozen climbs of 15 ft or so, admirable as a practice ground for young people in the area. After inspecting this I was taken on a search for more quarries hereabouts—there is reputed to be a considerable one from which the stone for Arundel Castle was obtained; we did not find it. This little discovery however does emphasise the great importance of minor rocks in a land where there is otherwise nothing and I feel sure that others equally worthy could be unearthed in similar situations by the diligent searcher.

We turn finally to the hills of the central Weald which, as we have said, are of Wealden Sandstone, the oldest rock formation exposed in this part of the country. These are known as the Forest Ridges and take the form of two slightly diverging hill lines running eastwards from the neighbourhood of Horsham. The first reaches close on 500 ft in the great forests of St Leonards, Tilgate and

Worth, even higher by Selfield Common and West Hoathly, and culminates in Ashdown Forest, where Crowborough Beacon is 787 ft. Though there are some fine sections with distant views, there is nevertheless very little impression of a continuous hill ridge. Most of the climbers' crags, described in the following chapter, are in this Forest Ridge area between Balcombe and Tunbridge Wells. Ashdown Forest is another piece of heath country, of which Cobbett wrote:

> It is a heath with here and there a few birch scrubs upon it, verily the most villainously ugly spot I ever saw in England. This lasts you for five miles, getting, if possible uglier and uglier all the way till, at last, as if barren soil, nasty spewy gravel, heath and even that stunted, were not enough, you see some rising spots, which instead of trees, present you with black, ragged, hideous rocks.

(The last part is believed to refer to the rocks at Uckfield.) This hill line continues through Rotherfield and Mark Cross to Wadhurst, where there are remains of ancient Wealden iron mines in Snape Wood; then on through Ticehurst to peter out gradually below the flat lands of Romney Marsh. The second Forest Ridge starts close to Lower Beeding and runs through Cuckfield to Haywards Heath. It disappears for some distance, though there are fine exposures of bare rock in the neighbourhood of Uckfield and Buxted, then reappears on the southern boundary of the Rother Valley. There are 500 ft hills by Cross-in-Hand and Heathfield, while Brightling Beacon reaches 647 ft; the line of the outcrop trends southwards to Battle and finishes in fine sea cliffs between Hastings and Pett Level, which will be detailed in a later chapter.

While some sections of these various sandstone ridges will provide obvious and entertaining short hill walks, for example in the Ide Hill, Leith Hill, Ashdown Forest or Black Down areas, there is little obvious scope for long-distance walking such as is available on the chalk. Such expeditions have to be contrived therefore, when needed. The walker could for example follow some of the ancient and Roman trackways in the steps of I. D. Margery, whose *Roman Ways in the Weald* is an admirable guide to where to go and what to see. The principal route is Stane Street, running from Chichester to London, the line of which has been known for many years. There are lesser ways, harder perhaps to trace, all mapped in detail in the above book—from London to Brighton and from London to Lewes, as well as cross-country tracks between them.

Other interesting local features in many parts of the central Weald are the remains of the iron working, which was carried out here roughly between Tudor times, when blast furnace processes came into use, and the 1700s, when coal began to emerge as a cheaper fuel and the industry moved north. The most conspicuous relics are the hammer ponds, the power from which was used for hammering and for blowing. The industry is recalled everywhere in the place names in which words like furnace, forge, hammer, etc, frequently occur. The iron was used for guns, examples of which can be found on Tower Wharf in London, for firebacks and grave-slabs. Camden has this to say of the Weald:

> Full of iron mines it is in sundry places, where for the making and fining thereof there be furnaces on every side, and a huge deale of wood is yearely spent, to which purpose divers brookes in many places are brought to runne in one chanell, and sundry medowes turned into pooles and waters, that they might bee of power sufficient to drive hammer milles, which beating upon the iron, resound all over the places adjoining.

The modern walker will perhaps be guided by E. Straker's *Wealden Iron*, of which there is a recent reprint. Another interesting trip might attempt to follow the Wey-Arun Canal, long since disused but still traceable for much of its length.

There would seem to be scope for a few point-to-point hill expeditions of the type popular elsewhere in Britain. For example the highest points in Sussex, Surrey and Kent, namely Black Down, Leith Hill and Betsom's Hill, are separated by crow-flight distances of 16 and 20 miles and thus could easily be covered in a day by an active walker. The Surrey 700s have also been suggested as a possibility. This expedition would begin at Gibbet Hill at Hindhead, proceed over Pitch and Holmbury Hills to Leith Hill, then cross Holmesdale to the North Downs at Hackhurst Downs above Gomshall. The remaining points are scattered along the line of the Downs—White Downs, west of the Dorking Gap, the edge above Betchworth chalk pit, Colley Hill at Reigate, points south of Caterham and finally the gradually rising line past Oxted and Titsey to the Kent border north-west of Westerham. The flying crow would make this one about 42 miles, but it would be somewhat further on the ground.

3

SANDSTONE CLIMBS

ONE day in 1601 a certain Lord North, out riding from Eridge House, came across a medicinal spring in the heart of the country-side; about it in the ensuing years grew Tunbridge Wells. At first it was only a small village near the spring—the wells near Tun-bridge—but as time went on it developed all the amenities of a popular spa. Among the local attractions the grotesque outcropping sandstone rocks protruded abundantly. As early as the 1630s Edmund Waller the poet featured them in his verses to Sacharissa (Lady Dorothy Sydney):

> To no human stock
> We owe this fierce unkindness, but the rock,
> That cloven rock, produced thee, by whose side
> Nature, to recompense the fatal pride
> Of such stern beauty, placed those healing springs
> Which not more help, than that destruction brings.

The springs are Nature's antidote to the troubles caused by the lady's charms!

More than a hundred years later Tunbridge Wells was a popular resort and we find Miss Elizabeth Carter writing to her friend Miss Catherine Talbot of the delights of visiting the High Rocks:

The Rocks themselves, shaded with trees and half overgrown with ivy, discover just enough of their own composition to give them the appearance of ruined buildings; and reminded us of the romantic descriptions of the abode of the Enchanters. We drank tea in this wild region after sunset; and then waited to see the effect of moon-light on so solemn a scene; this was extremely fine and so very amusing that we did not get back till a good while after ten.

The weird Toad Rock on the common was another well-visited curiosity, and great was the speculation in pre-geological times about its probable origin. However during the nineteenth century the larger processes by which the Weald had been wrought and

49

the detailed processes which accounted for the outcropping sand-stone came to be understood. These were all described by Topley in his *Geology of the Weald* in 1875, where Harrison's Rocks and 'Rocks near Buxted', probably Hermitage Rocks, were figured for all to see. Meanwhile ordinary travellers passed by and marvelled. Martell in 1822 wrote of 'a fine lake overhung with sandstone rock near the seat of the Earl of Sheffield in the parish of Fletching'— but no substantial rocks have ever been discovered there; now these pleasant grounds are open to the public through the National Trust. On his rides William Cobbett frequently passed through this countryside; on the side of the road from Turner's Hill to Lindfield he noted:

> . . . a long chain of rocks, or, rather, rocky hills, with trees grow-ing amongst the rocks, or, apparently out of them, as they do in the woods near Ross in Herefordshire, and as they do in the Blue Mountains in America, where you can see no earth at all; where all seems rock, and yet where the trees grow most beautifully.

He goes on to mention the very remarkable detached pinnacle of Great-upon-Little, a sandstone block standing on a narrow stalk, which is over against one of these rock walls amongst the trees.

The earlier mountaineers, those stalwarts who formed the Alpine Club in its earliest days, knew nothing of the Wealden rocks. It is said that Martin Conway, afterwards a prominent mountaineer in all parts of the world, began his climbing career on the rocks on Rusthall Common; with his eyes firmly set on the great ranges it is unlikely that he came back in his mature years. However, three routes at Bull's Hollow have been named for him. In the 1890s

———

(above) Selborne from the Hanger. Village home of the eighteenth-century naturalist, Gilbert White; still largely unspoilt; *(below)* Toad Rock, Tunbridge Wells, a fine example of the grotesque forms taken on by weathered sandstone. It has been climbed but should be regarded as out-of-bounds to climbers

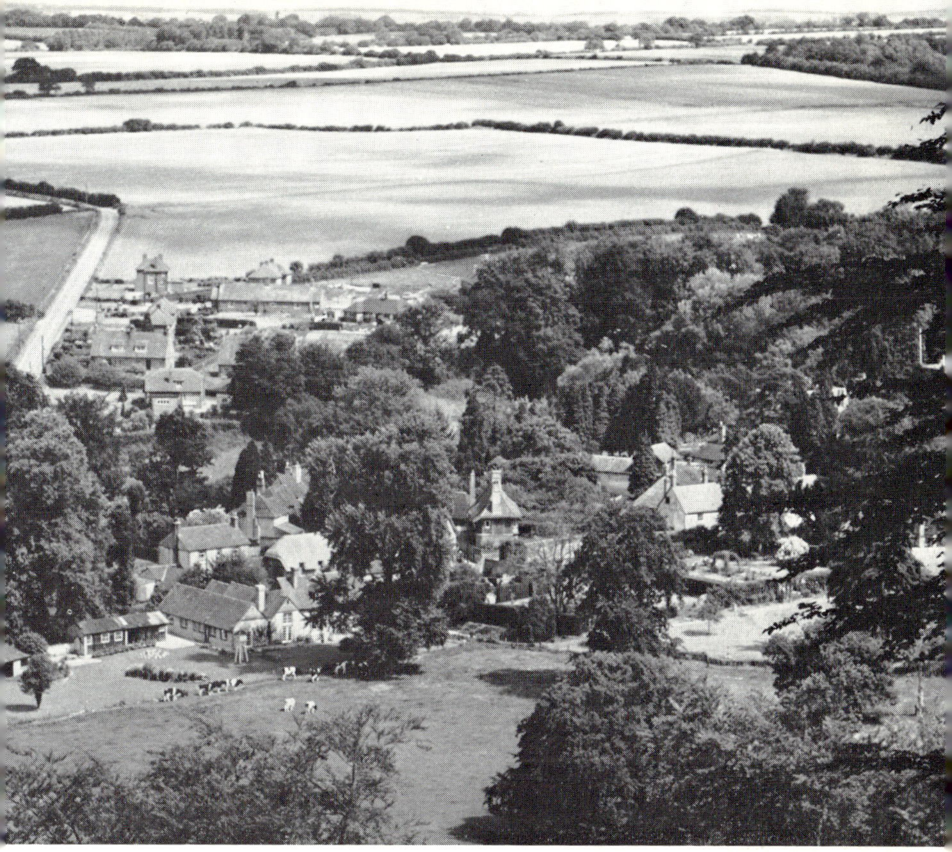

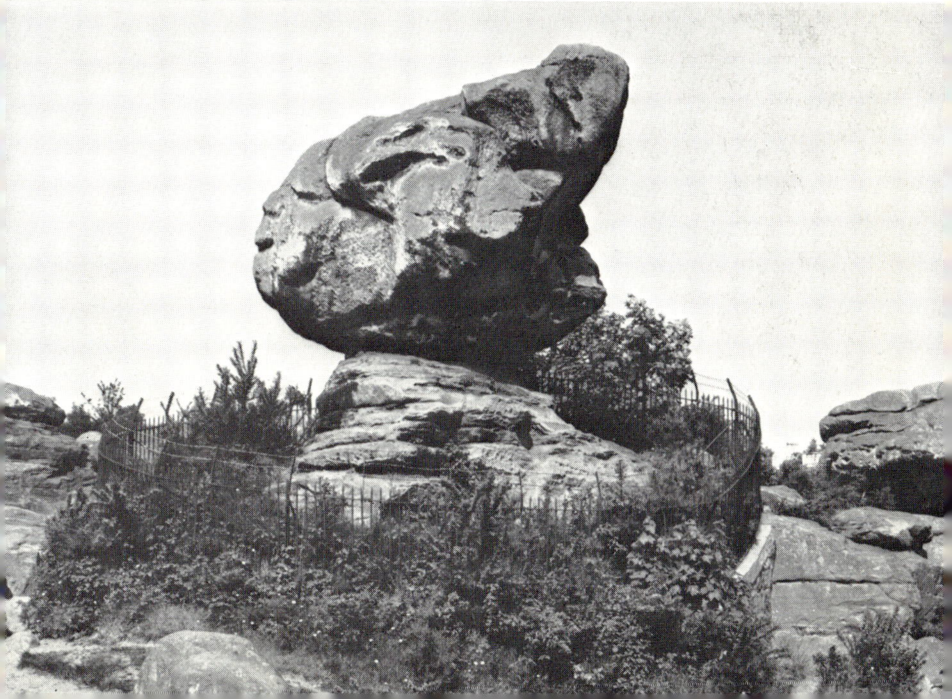

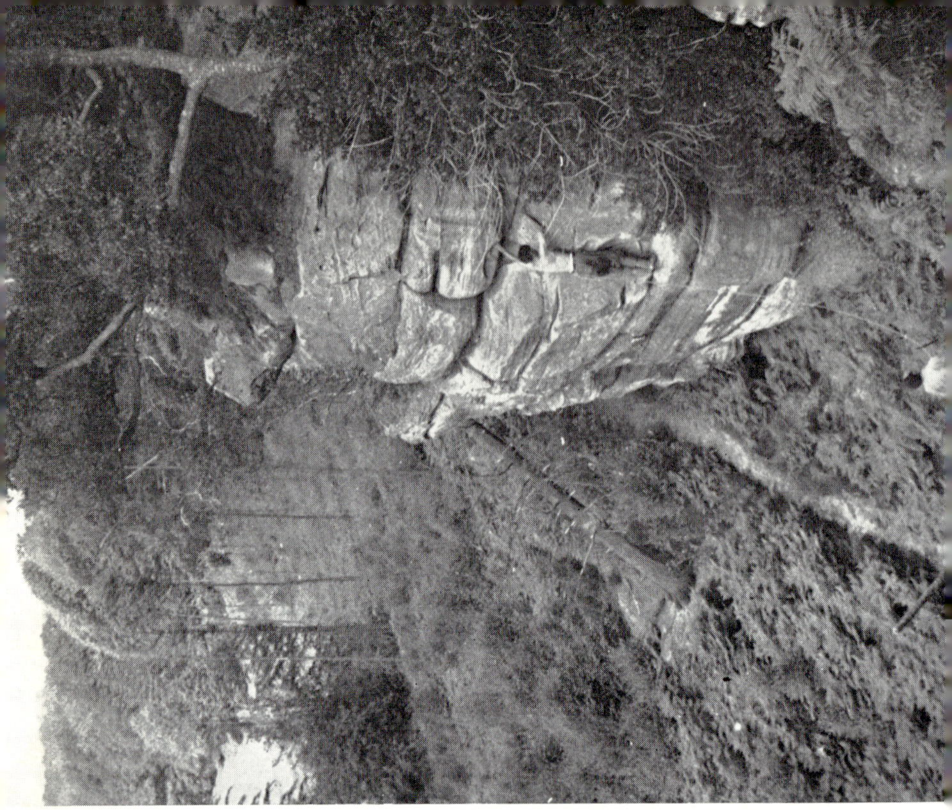

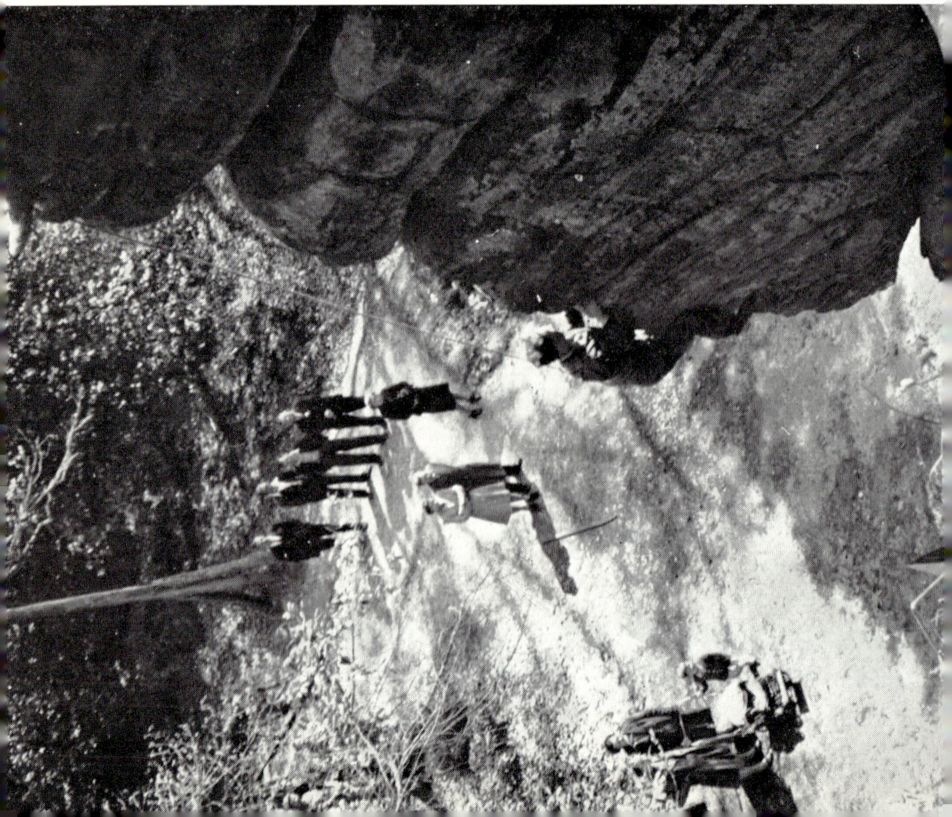

Owen Glynne Jones, passing by as we have said on his bicycle, cannot have realised how close he was to rocks which would have exercised him even more appropriately for his zealous climbing programme; otherwise he might have advanced Wealden climbing history by more than thirty years. The rocks slumbered on; alpinists Charles Nettleton and Claude Wilson lived close by at Tunbridge Wells and indeed the first sighting of Harrison's Rocks by a climber took place in 1908 when the former passed along the valley below with the Eridge Hunt. The two of them returned for another look but it is uncertain whether they climbed anything.

So the rocks remained just a picturesque background to the lowland scenery; for example, E. V. Lucas wrote of his boyhood:

. . . our favourite district was Buxted, because of the rocks there; great fat smooth grey rocks, like elephant's backs.

Of the rocks at Tunbridge Wells, he says:

The Toad is free; the High Rocks, however, can be inspected by the curious only on payment of an entrance fee . . . the rocks appear more unreal than any rocks ever seen upon the stage. Freed from their pleasure garden surroundings they would become beautifully wild and romantic and tropically un-English; but as it is, with their notice boards and bridges, they are disappointing, except of course to children. . . . Finer rocks, because more remote and free from labels and tea rooms, are those known as Penn's Rocks, three miles to the south-west, in a beautiful valley.

The climbing breakthrough came in 1926 when the possibilities of the various local rocks were realised by Miss N. E. Barnard (later Mrs N. E. Morin) of Tunbridge Wells, who had climbed on

---

(left) High Rocks, Tunbridge Wells. Frank Elliott is climbing Swing Face of Hut Boulder before a Sunday afternoon audience (mid-1940s); (right) Harrison's Rocks, Groombridge. The climb: Moonlight Arête; the climbers: G. Scott Johnstone and Charles Ellis; the period: mid-1940s. There was more vegetation around in those days

D

similar outcrops near Paris with members of the Groupe de Haute Montagne. The earliest routes were made at High Rocks and Harrison's Rocks. During the 1930s the latter outcrop was adopted by the Mountaineering Section of the Camping Club of Great Britain and Ireland, who proclaimed themselves as having 'access to the only grounds within easy reach of London where rock climbing practice can be obtained'. The first guidebook, by M. O. Sheffield and H. Courtney Bryson of that club, which appeared in 1934, listed around thirty climbs; but the circulation was small and the outcrops continued for the moment to rest, still relatively undisturbed, in the Sussex countryside.

Meanwhile Courtney Bryson set out to explore other rocks in the area and in 1936 produced his *Rock Climbs Round London*—a revelation to those of us who were just starting to climb at that time. Though I did not think so then, I am convinced now that this is the ideal outcrop climbing guidebook, perfectly appropriate to the status of its subject. One cannot, or should not, treat little rocks like these in flat country as though they were mountains; as Bryson says:

> . . . the enlarged boulder problems described hereafter are pranks —practice pitches, performed *faute de mieux*, and proceed from the light-hearted joy which exists in the hearts of those who love mountains and think of them often. It is true that every time you get up a difficult pitch you have succeeded in life; but he who thinks that this is mountaineering is a synecdochist, substituting a small part for the whole.

Overboard goes the surgical precision of the usual climbers' guidebook with statements like: 'the time sacrificing ceremony of correlation has been cunningly circumvented by omission of complex cases'. For one climb he recommends white ducks, for another insouciance and glue, for a third, 'an undignified wriggle of a climb', 'if you have embonpoint be a spectator rather than a participator'; the whole adds up to a delightful and in those days most inspiring book. So under Bryson's literary guidance we began our own explorations. During 1936 it took us to Stone Farm (I still remember the excitement aroused by my first sight of this fine outcrop); it took us also to the dark recesses of Bull's Hollow and High Rocks Annexe and the classical ground at Harrison's Rocks. Soon a small group of us founded the London end of the Polaris Mountaineering Club, a southern/Midland group which has survived to this day. We began the exploration of High Rocks, where Bryson had not recorded any climbs; London members put up several easy routes but it was Bernard Simmonds from Nottingham who in the course of business visits to London really showed us what was possible. Anaconda Chimney and Simian Progress (the latter named obliquely for him) at High Rocks and Stone Farm Chimney were first leads of his. Except at Harrison's Rocks one seldom met with other climbers, though it is recorded that Oxford University enthusiasts sometimes came to High Rocks in this period. Then at Stone Farm I met three members of a newly-formed club (the London Association of the Junior Mountaineering Club of Scotland), a group which I was subsequently to join and under whose banner the major guide-writing of future years was to be carried out.

Between 1940 and 1947, when my first guidebook to the rocks was published, I was lucky enough to be associated with all the major developments. During much of these war years odd hours snatched here were the only climbing activity, the participants being either members of the JMCS or other close friends. Outstanding was Frank Elliott, already a leading gritstone climber with a route at Cratcliff Tor in Derbyshire named for him—Elliott's Unconquerable; he contributed North Wall and Swing Face at High Rocks, Centurion's Groove at Bull's Hollow, Ashdown and Cat Walls at Stone Farm, Wildcat Wall at Harrison's and Twin and Tiger Slabs at Eridge. Outstanding too was Clifford Fenner, a forester from Hawkhurst, whose new routes at Harrison's included the even more difficult Slim Finger Crack, Niblick and Monkey's Necklace. As a reaction against the flippant style of Courtney Bryson my *Sandstone Climbs in South East England* was a straightforward piece of guidebook-writing, adequate but possibly rather ponderous in view of the insignificance of the subject. It owed a great deal to some magnificent plans of the various crags surveyed and drawn by Edward Zenthon, who was himself a very competent rock climber. The club acted as publishers.

Soon the post-war boom was upon us. As the numbers at the rocks increased so it became more and more difficult, and finally impossible, to keep pace with the developments. Notable newcomers in this period were the Sandstone Climbing Club who for a period used a building in the grounds of High Rocks as a hut and from it made some quite startling innovations among the routes. Parties from Tunbridge Wells under the guidance of the evergreen Mrs

N. E. Morin were often seen around. The Climbers' Club took over the guidebook in 1956, calling it *South East England*, and I was once again the author. My aim this time was to mention all outcrops everywhere and to this end I searched through every sheet of two editions of the Six-Inch Ordnance Survey Map for shading suggestive of rock. My friend Charles Kemp then drove me all over Sussex, south Surrey and west Kent visiting all the places; we came up with one excellent outcrop previously unknown to us, Bowles Rocks at Eridge, as well as a good many lesser. A new edition was called for in 1964 but by now I was so far out of the main stream that, though my original text was still broadly adequate, information on new climbs had to be supplied by two extremely competent young London climbers, David Fagan and John Smoker. The number of climbers increases every year, so that nowadays Harrison's Rocks on a fine Sunday are seriously over-crowded. You will even find climbers there on a mid-week day out of season. A new edition of the guidebook (revised by L. E. and L. R. Holliwell) has recently been issued by the Climbers' Club.

This overcrowding saddens me for I wonder to what extent I am responsible for it. All of these visitors have my guidebook in their hand, if not literally, at least figuratively; the alternative is not however no guidebook but someone else's so that the present state of affairs would have come about anyway. Solitude, that quiet-ness of surroundings which attracted me originally to climbing, is fast disappearing. The up-and-coming enthusiast in fact no longer expects it; for him climbing is a sport carried out in much company, a spectator sport if you like. It brings excitement, adventure and outdoor life to the many so that it is no bad thing that it should be so popular, even if this sacrifices certain essential features of climbing in times past. Solitude can still be found but it is further afield and more elusive than before.

The Wealden outcrops are unimpressive, often partly hidden by trees; only at Stone Farm, not by any means the highest, are the rocks so sited that they dominate the landscape. The colour varies from a pale grey on dry faces exposed to the sun to a greyish black, often smeared with the greens and oranges of moss and lichen when heavily shaded by trees. Local changes of colour and climb-ability take place from decade to decade as trees grow and fall. The material is sound enough to climb upon, yet it is in fact no more than a compacted sand with surface hardened by exposure to the atmosphere. A boulder thrown against the wall breaks, not into fragments, but into grains of sand. The faces consist largely of bulges with rounded horizontal ledges between; there are deep vertical cracks which in places become passages separating detached blocks from the main wall of the outcrop. The holds, invariably sloping and rounded, accumulate sand which has sometimes to be wiped clear before they can be used safely. Such is the softness of the rock that such cleaning can merge fairly readily into abrasive enlargement. A big satisfying pocket hold usually rates special mention in the account of a climb, for instance Courtney Bryson: 'hook two fingers into the minute triangular hold' or from one of my own descriptions: 'there is one hold like a gigantic handle which is used all the way up'. Wind-eroded pockets often retain a slender strip of rock at the front giving a hold like a cup handle which is completely unreliable. Almost all climbs are single pitch; belays are few, usually tree trunks or roots at the top, the rope from which rapidly abraids deep slots in the soft rock, slots which eventually give a castellated look to the outline. From the point of view of training the novice, the arrangement of low rocks with trees along the top is particularly appropriate as the rope can be run through a sling attached to a tree and back to the bottom and the instructor can indicate points of style, holds and so on to his pupil, while still taking in the slack and supporting him as he climbs. It should perhaps be added, however, that this is not good rock on which to learn to climb; granite and mountain rocks in general have square and incut ledges and holds, at any rate on the easier climbs, which conform much more closely to the layman picture of what a hold should be. For experienced climbers it provides an excellent physical training but, as the harder routes are seldom led, the mental training is less adequate.

It is now time to take a closer look at some of the major outcrops.

Harrison's Rocks, the most widely known of the Wealden outcrops, line the western edge of Birchden Wood between Groombridge and Eridge Stations. The origin of the name is lost to us. The valley below has a flat floor, threaded by stream, road and railway, steep slopes sweep up to the foot of the rocks, above which the summit land is more or less flat once again. Trees are plentiful though there have been extensive clearances of recent years; now many parts stand out with the light grey of sun-dried rock. Forge

Farm, the name of which recalls its former connections with iron working, has oast houses providing an essentially local background. The outcrop is L-shaped in plan, some 500 yd facing west and 150 yd facing south; it just exceeds 30 ft in the highest places. There are three detached summits—the Isolated Buttress, the Squat Tower and North Boulder. The conditions for access have changed repeatedly since climbing began there. In the early days of obvious private ownership visits were only allowed on certain days of the week; for a period it was necessary to obtain a permit in advance for every visit; later the owner of Forge Farm permitted access at any time subject to certain restrictions about climbing close behind the house. The large numbers of post-war climbers aggravated the problem; eventually the Forestry Commission bought Birchden Wood, the entrance at Forge Farm was closed and entry had to be made through the wood itself from Groombridge. At times there have been threats of closure and these continue even today. At one time the proposal to use the outcrop as the back wall to a series of pig pens was reported in the national press. Recently all these troubles seem to have been settled for the outcrop now belongs to the British Mountaineering Council and is held in trust by the Central Council for Physical Recreation; the Forestry Commission, however, which owns the surrounding land, has made certain conditions which have to be closely observed—no camping, bivouacing, fires, stoves, litter, pitons, vibrams or nailed boots, no obstruction by parked cars and access only from the Groombridge end. No one knows how soon it may change again.

Climbing development here has taken place steadily with hardly any of the sudden leaps forward which characterise the story at other places. The Bryson and Sheffield guidebook listed 30 routes, *Rock Climbs Round London*, 45, *Sandstone Climbs in South East England*, 110, the 1956 edition just over 150, the 1963 edition 170. Now there are more than 200. The Girdle Traverse, carried out by E. R. Zenthon in 1941, was an outstanding achievement. The rocks are so low that the climber is forced from time to time to the top or the bottom; otherwise the route gives over 1,000 ft of horizontal climbing of exceptional interest. By 1947 all the easier lines had been worked out and the additions of the last two decades represent advances in the general technique of climbing everywhere. What are the classic routes of the crag? Many would plump for the Isolated Buttress Climb, of which Bryson wrote:

Now, if tall, exercise your prerogative and stretch for the flat knob; if short, monkey up the arête; if debonair, lay back; if grammatical, lie back. Use the small tree at which the breath is recovered as a foot hold. It bends gracefully. Treat it delicately. It will collapse one day.

The tree did collapse, was mended for a time with insulating tape, and finally disappeared altogether; the constant passage of ascending hands and feet ensures that there will never be another. So-called Long Layback is also an entertainment, the upper part is a right-angled corner where the climber finds himself with his back on the left wall facing outwards and contemplating a very high step on to a hold on the right wall, which can only be reached by placing the foot on the hold with the hand.

The names too are interesting. The originals used by the Morins were superseded by Bryson's nomenclature, which he imposed by means of his guidebook. We inherited this basic network and built on it. To avoid personal names we sometimes used allusive names for climbs, which gave them a personal tag as far as our immediate circle was concerned; thus Forester's Wall is named for Clifford Fenner, who followed that profession; Blue Peter commemorates a certain Tunbridge Wells schoolmaster who always climbed in a blue boiler-suit. Downfall was really Elliott's Downfall because in a careless moment he fell spectacularly from it in the early days of its history.

Nowadays Harrison's Rocks have a somewhat worn look, the top edge scored with rope grooves, the vegetation below trampled by circumambulatory feet, a desolate look of over-use. But the rocks change less with time than we ourselves do; certainly new generations still find in them, just as we did thirty years ago, the same adventure and excitement, the same inspiration. Let us hope they will continue to fulfil this role for many years to come. One can go with the guidebook and become steeped in the traditions of the place. Alternatively one could set out without it as though this were still a new adventure and discover and name all the routes for oneself with complete unconcern as to what has gone before. It would be interesting indeed to hear that someone had done just this.

High Rocks, situated on either side of a small valley close to High Rocks Hotel 2 miles west of Tunbridge Wells, though not so well-known to climbers in general, are of an importance comparable with Harrison's Rocks. The main part of the outcrop, which reaches to just over 40 ft, is a pleasure ground attached to the hotel; there is a charge for entry and a further charge for climbers. The rock wall continues outside the boundary fence for some distance—the Continuation Wall—and reappears on the far side of the valley in High Rocks Annexe, or Bristol Jack's. There are four isolated summits, the Hut, Slab and Isolated Boulders in the grounds and the Steeple in front of the Continuation Wall; some other detached blocks which would otherwise be inaccessible are reached by rustic bridges provided for the sightseers.

Here Bryson really passed on the exploration to his successors:

As implied, these are the highest rocks in this part of the country. For the sum of twopence a pithy and succinct guide, full of history and geology and poppycockology, may be purchased where, modestly as a newspaper extolling its own merits, it is stated that the High Rocks are 'unsurpassed by any other beauty spot in England'. In addition to climbing you may plunge into a reckless round of gaiety for 'there is no limit to the time allowed for occupying the swings, and the visitor, having once paid for admission to the grounds (6d), is allowed to stay as long as he chooses'. Exhilarated by the swings, bewildered by the Maze, fascinated by the lake, deafened by the Bell Rock, confident in the powers of the Wishing Rock, and awed by the Warning Rock, you will probably be so bereft of emotion that the mere scaling of faces 'rising high in the air, mingling with and o'ertopping the trees', will savour of bathos. If after sampling all the delights, you still have sufficient energy left to climb, there is a large number of worth-while climbs to be had, scattered over the wide area occupied by the huge broken-up blocks of rock. High Rocks are conspicuous for sheer flat rock faces. Many are undercut, rendering a start from the ground impossible, but difficult traverses

———

Page 61
Beachy Head, taken from the west looking back towards the lighthouse. The climbing area is further on, round the corner

Page 62
Climbers on Beachy Head, 1894—the famous Devil's Chimney. Aleister Crowley is seen on the Needle, with G. Grant nearer at hand on the Tooth. The whole of this mass fell into the sea in the mid-1950s

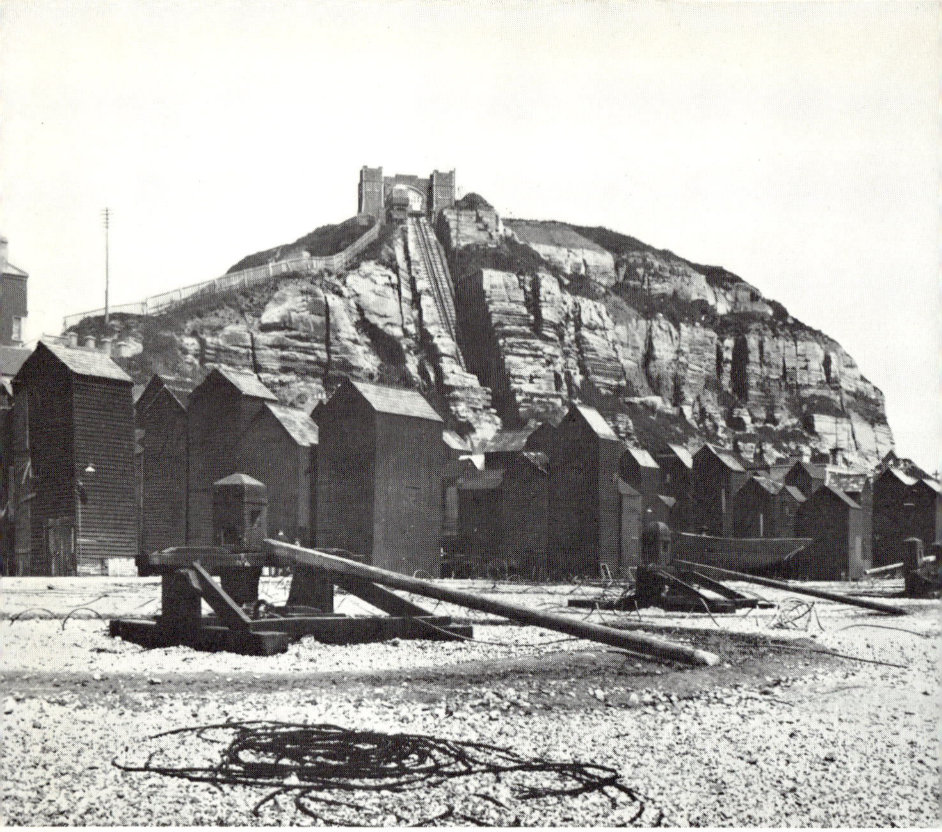

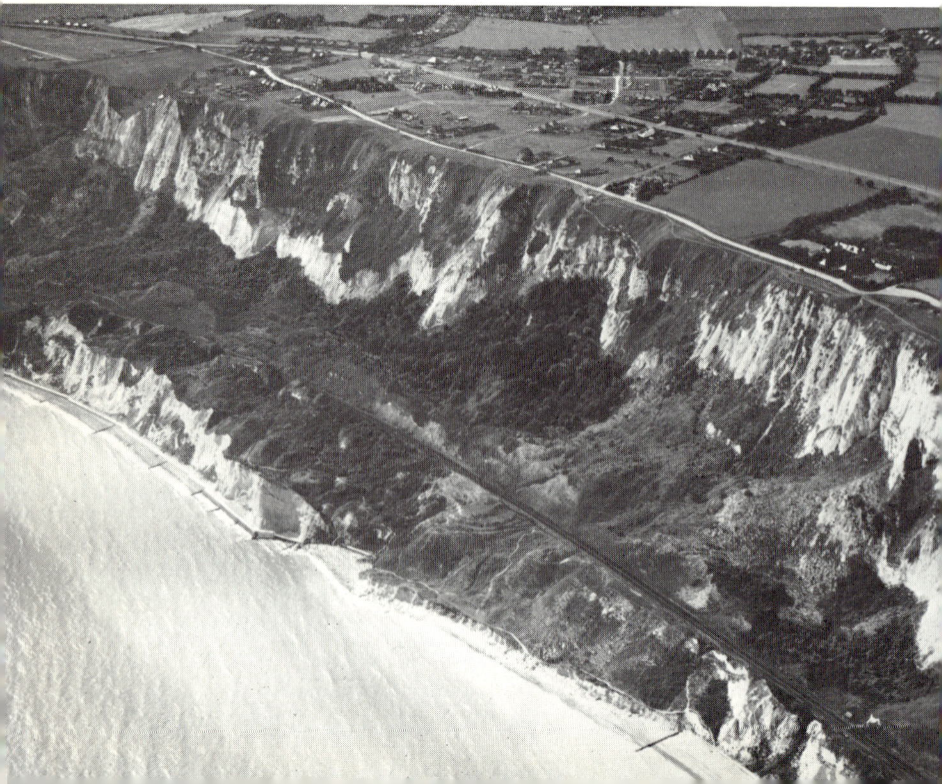

near the tops are practicable in some cases, though a rope may be necessary to reach them. Many of the rock faces are parallel, forming corridors three to five feet wide which may be chimneyed up by those with sufficient push to last the seventy feet.

Even after we had found out that he had overestimated the height by a factor of two, the prospects were still entrancing and occupied us for many exciting years of exploration. By 1947 there were 95 routes, in 1956 120 and in 1963 over 200. The new guidebook lists 217.

The smooth chimneys of High Rocks are its speciality; there is possibly nowhere else in Britain where such a range of practice can be obtained. All possible widths are available and we were able to develop techniques for climbing them which proved invaluable when tackling chimneys in other types of rock. Thus when climbing regularly at High Rocks I found no difficulty at all with the outside edge route on the Monolith Crack in North Wales (rated by us as 'much easier than Anaconda Chimney'), a route with a reasonable reputation. Years after my High Rocks days, confronted with the parallel flakes of Bear Rock at Hartland Quay, I recognised immediately the familiar chimney form; alas, I no longer had the push to tackle it.

Each of the smooth chimney techniques is based on having two entirely independent systems for wedging the body in the cleft; these systems are used alternately, one supporting the body while the other is being moved to a higher position. Consider first a smooth chimney just narrow enough to admit the body. The wedges involve alternate use of feet (toes on front wall, heels on back) and arms (elbows on back wall, palms of hands, fingers downwards,

---

Page 63

Climbers on Beachy Head, 1969. Tom Patey traverses out towards Etheldreda's Pinnacle, first climbed by Crowley in 1894 and still standing

Page 64

(above) East Hill, Hastings. Massive outcrops of Wealden Sandstone rise above the ancient fishermen's huts in the old town. There is no record of climbing because everything is too public and too rotten; *(below)* the Warren, Folkestone, otherwise known as Little Switzerland. A landslip area with rock walls, caves, etc, threaded by the main-line railway between Folkestone and Dover

on the front). Here the problem is often that of moving the chest upwards against the friction of the walls. When the cleft is slightly wider the wedges involve alternate use of legs (heels on back wall, knees on front) and arms (used as before). When it is no longer possible to span the cleft between knees and heels the supporting wedge is taken between knees on the front wall and back on the back. Movement upwards is contrived by putting one foot on the wall behind, pushing one's back off the wall to raise it, then returning that same leg to the front wall in a higher position. The operation is then repeated with the other leg. When the cleft becomes so wide that it cannot be spanned between knee and back, the supporting wedge uses back on one wall and both feet flat on the other. The back can be raised by pushing it off from the wall with the hands, the feet walking correspondingly upwards immediately afterwards; or the feet can be placed alternately on the wall behind as in the previous method. These four techniques cover clefts of all possible widths and their application by a particular individual depends entirely on his length of limb. All involve facing one way or the other in the cleft, the choice often being determined by the existence and possible utilisation of rest ledges. There are two further techniques in which the climber faces outwards or inwards rather than sideways. In a reasonably narrow cleft another purely wedging method uses the upper thighs pressing one on either wall, alternating with the shoulders and upper arms pressing similarly. A wider cleft with some side ledges can be climbed by the well-known technique of bridging, where holds for hands and feet are taken on either wall as required.

A feature of these rocks in the pre-war era was the plank swing, part of the amenities of the pleasure ground. This consisted of a 10 ft plank, 1 ft wide and 3 in thick, supported by hinged steel rods and chains at each end and hung from a massive timber support. You hooked your heels behind the end of the plank, held the upright supports one in each hand, kicked off and drove it higher and higher by vigorous leg pushes. Once the plank and its load were on the move it was absolutely vital to hang on tightly; as it was only 1–2 in above the ground, anyone falling off would have been ground to powder or at least have suffered serious breakages. Somehow this never happened. Now it is many years gone.

Here we had no nomenclature to work from and except for

certain features named by tradition, had a completely free hand. The problem was to name a series of clefts which initially were designated 'a', 'b', 'c', etc. The suggestion that each one should be named for a famous mountaineer having the same initial letter was seriously considered, though we felt that we should have to approach contemporaries for their permission before doing so. Then when contemplating one day the serious contortions necessary in the ascents, we were struck with the idea that snakes would have suitable bodies and muscles for the job, so the chimneys became snakes of the same initial letters—Anaconda, Boa, Cobra etc.

The classic climbs are Anaconda Chimney, a veritable test piece for the chimney climber, Chockstone Chimney and the first three routes on the Isolated Boulder—Simian Progress, North Wall and the Ordinary Route. Port Crack on Continuation Wall and Valhalla Wall on the Annexe are also very worthy.

During the 1950s the Sandstone Climbing Club more than doubled the number of routes, producing some fearsome lines such as Pussy-foot, Advertisement Wall, Pinchgrip, Bludnok Wall, Tilley Lamp etc, which were harder than anything else on Wealden sandstone. I do not know the philosophy behind their nomenclature. The leaders of this wave were P. Gordon, W. Maxwell and John Smoker, but it is the all-round high standard of a group like this which really stimulates the technical advances. Certainly they set sandstone standards as high as those of any other rock type in the country. Among the many very fine climbers of more recent years, Martin Boysen has been perhaps the outstanding innovator.

High Rocks have not changed much throughout the years. The state of the vegetation and the trees is static so that the scenic amenities are well preserved; this is a good thing. Anyone who wishes to develop or to maintain a technique of chimney climbing, or to see the ultimate of what is possible on sandstone, is certainly recommended to go to High Rocks, where he will have to pay a special entrance fee for climbers. The Continuation Wall and the Annexe are both on private land; the former seems to be reasonably accessible at present, though there is no formal permission to climb; access to the latter is more or less forbidden. Certainly both have their points of interest.

Eridge Rocks, behind the church at Eridge Green, are equidistant from High Rocks and Harrison's Rocks. This splendid outcrop above a grassy ride in a lonely woodland of high trees and bluebells was quietly and unobtrusively enjoyed for a decade. It was here that the post-war boomers did us all a great disservice, for singing, shouting and the lighting of fires during the course of climbing visits led to an abrupt closure of the rocks and they have stayed closed ever since. Courtney Bryson missed out on this one also: 'if their climbing facilities equalled their beauty, this spot would be paradise'. One can only conclude that he had not seen the whole of it. Indeed on our first two or three visits, misled by his pessimism, we only saw the part nearest the entrance where there is a wall with some chimneys reminiscent of High Rocks. The rocks peter out for a time, there is a big S bend in the track, then 200 yd beyond starts the main part of the outcrop. It reaches 30 ft in places, but there are no detached summits; the tally of routes in 1947 was 45 but more are said to have been added since.

All these fine climbs belong to the past, but we can still recall with pleasure Eridge Tower with its three splendid routes, Twin and Tiger Slabs and so on. Of particular interest is Amphitheatre Crack, a narrow cleft which can be climbed to a certain height inside and then becomes too narrow for further progress. We decided to use the same tactics as the pioneers on Flake Crack on Scafell Central Buttress—an inserted chockstone, a climber outside the crack sitting in rope slings attached thereto and a second climber using the first as foothold to reach the upper part. Local rock proved to be too soft for the job. Then a short time later, as we crossed a stream on the way home from Dow Crag at Coniston, someone suggested taking home a suitable chock from the stream bed. The following weekend Amphitheatre Crack was climbed using this wedged boulder of mountain rock, carefully imported from the Lake District, and there it remains still.

There are a number of interesting exposures of sandstone on the commons around Tunbridge Wells. Wellington Rocks in the town itself are suitable only for very young climbers. A short way off on Rusthall Common the rocks are more imposing; Courtney Bryson devoted a section to Bull's Hollow, commenting particularly on the seclusion:

> The trees guard the calm ease of the expert from the curious gaze of an unappreciative public, and decently veil the frantic antics of the peripatetic tyro from juvenile hilarity. A human belay on top of the rocks sometimes attracts attention on fine Sundays.

He described 8 climbs; by 1963 there were 24; now there are 45. It is a little hard to account for his enthusiasm. It is in fact a quaggy dump—the rocks, which reach nearly 30 ft, are probably the walls of an ex-quarry and are thus of doubtful quality. A few hundred yards away in the village of Denny Bottom is the famous Toad Rock, which has been climbed, though not often, as it must be regarded as out-of-bounds to climbers. Almost in the front garden of a nearby house is Denny Bottom Pinnacle another isolated summit of some merit in an unusually public site. Rock walls, detached blocks and sand are all plentiful hereabouts, though it is too much in the public eye for climbing exploration to be seriously possible. Happy Valley Rocks, by St Paul's Church, also on Rusthall Common are negligible except for another isolated pinnacle.

The big search through the Six-Inch Ordnance Maps which I did for the 1956 guidebook produced a fine discovery in Bowles Rocks, 1 mile south of Eridge Station. I think they were already known to the Tunbridge Wells group who had so far kept discreetly silent. This outcrop, though not as long as Harrison's, is almost as high as High Rocks in places. On our first visit we found it being used as the back wall of a series of pig sties; the monstrous porkers in residence had consumed every piece of greenstuff within reach, leaving a typically desert landscape at the rock foot. Their fierce snuffling and the fearful smell barred off the climbing most effectively and we did none of it. Thus the 1956 guidebook confined itself to the promise: 'if these conditions should change at some future date the outcrop would be an excellent prospect'. The changes came shortly afterwards, the pigs departed and were replaced by the splendours of Bowles Mountaineering Gymnasium. Over the years this was gradually built up as a climbing school offering rock climbing courses to all age groups, including youth organisations, on various days of the week. There is camping, bivouacing and Alpine hut accommodation, club house, swimming pool, children's playground, cable railway and chapel, with about 100 rock climbs alongside—a thoroughly delightful place. Currently it is known as Bowles Outdoor Pursuit Centre. Immediately to the north by the main road there are other rocks at Boarshead. Pelton in the *Guide to Tunbridge Wells* says that it is named for 'a huge high stone, capped with another one like a monstrous head—a frightful figure, a sort of Druid Idol'.

Stone Farm with its pleasant open situation is perhaps the most delightful of the Wealden outcrops. The rocks line the top of a bracken- and grass-covered hillside which slopes down to the broad valley of the infant Medway. This valley, stretching away eastwards and formerly meadows and farmland, has of recent years been inundated to form a reservoir for Crawley New Town. The dam is miles out of sight up at Forest Row, so that this end of the lake looks completely natural; with the rocks and the bracken one might almost be on the outskirts of the Lake District. The rocks barely reach 25 ft though there are now more than 50 climbs; the pleasing light-grey of sun-dried sandstone is very much in evidence. There are two isolated summits—Stone Farm Pinnacle and the Inaccessible Boulder (which of course isn't).

Courtney Bryson mentioned the outcrop but did not record any climbs so that we determined the entire nomenclature. One of the classic routes is Stone Farm Chimney—a climbing dilemma. There is a bulge inside which stops the climber from pushing his body up in safety inside the comforting walls. To get higher without excessive effort he must move outside more and more as he ascends and, as he does so, the feeling of imminence of fall-off increases steadily. The balance point between upward progress and falling out has to be approached fairly closely in this case, so that the climb is more a matter of confidence than of ability. When you do it often it is easy but at other isolated times it can be very difficult indeed. Nearby is Cat Wall named in this case, not for the feline attributes needed to surmount it, but for the Cat Inn at West Hoathly, where very pleasant draught cider used to close the day's climbing. The village church spire can be seen on the far skyline of the valley.

Access has always been unhindered even though the rocks are on private land. During the last few years the owner has had to bar entry to the lane along the top, as so-called mountaineers were driving their cars along it to save the 100 yd walk from the road. It is puzzling to know how such people ever get very far on their mountains. If the differences become too serious we could, as at Eridge Green, lose it altogether and this would be a serious and shameful affair for southern climbers.

It can be seen that the major rock outcrops all lie in a belt stretching westwards from Tunbridge Wells to just beyond East Grinstead. In this same area there are a number of other sites which have not been developed for climbing, usually because they are on private land and inaccessible. For example, there are unattainable rocks in the grounds of Glen Andred and Leyswood which face Harrison's Rocks across the valley. Then a little further west is the fine outcrop of Penn's Rocks; all is on private land though some of the lesser boulders are close to a public footpath. Courtney Bryson seems to have visited the finest light-grey rocks which can be seen at a distance near the house, for he says, 'many fine climbs averaging thirty feet are to be found there, especially on the two western boulders gorgonised by lupus-stricken Giant Ugly, with a face ten feet high'. It sounds as though this may be another isolated summit, while there is certainly one, called Penn's Approach Pinnacle, in the woods near the Groombridge road.

There are rocks at Ashurst Wood, $1\frac{1}{2}$ miles south-east of East Grinstead. The accessible part is an ex-quarry and not particularly promising, but the outcrop stretches on either hand into private land and there is a pinnacle to the south. Some climbs have been done says Courtney Bryson 'near a ravine which acts as a repository for ancient and indiscreet articles of domestic utility'.

As William Cobbett noticed in passing, there are rocks on either side of the Turner's Hill to Haywards Heath road, 2 miles south of the former. In Chiddingly Wood divided between the estates of Philpots and Stonehurst is one of the finest outcrops in southern England, useless however to climbers as it is largely inaccessible, and the rocks are blanketed with trees above and below. Here is the famous Great-upon-Little, a massive cubic block standing on a small plinth with overhangs all round; it is easily surmounted however by jumping across from the top of the adjacent rock wall. It was described and figured by Thomas Pownall in *Archaeologia* in 1779; Cobbett and Mantell referred to it; Topley figured it; in fact it has always been a well-known, though probably little-visited, curiosity. The valley below, says *Ghosts over England*, is a 'terrible ellynge place', haunted by a 'gurt black ghost hound' called Gytrack. There are other rocks near the road; west of the road Long Wood has an extensive exposure of sandstone mostly low, though up to 20 ft high in places; this is now included in the Wakehurst Place property of the National Trust and is open for inspection though not for climbing.

There are some minor rock sites to the north of the main area notably around Chiddingstone and Cowden. Behind the half-timbered houses in the former village is the Chidding Stone, described by the author of *Highways and Byways* as a 'Druidical judgment seat'. It is hardly climbworthy. Opposite Rocks Inn at Chiddingstone Hoath there is a small outcrop forming the back wall of some allotments. Here says Courtney Bryson at his most sprightly:

> The assaults on Nature in her more rugged aspects will be viewed by a disdainful cock, proudly strutting his dames before. The animal audience is likely to be reinforced by one of the lords of creation arrayed as a yokel peregrinating from the neighbouring Rocks Inn.

This may well have happened to him. Close-by at Stonewall Park is another inaccessible outcrop, only just off the edge of the road. The rocks at Redleaf House, near Penshurst Station, not of course open to the public, are said to have delighted Landseer and Turner.

Several fine outcrops are known to the south of the main area around Uckfield and Mayfield. Perhaps the most interesting are the 'rocks near Rocks Farm, Buxted' figured by Topley, probably though not certainly the fine exposure of sandstone in the gardens of Hermitage. This, which can be seen over the fence from a public footpath, represents, I may say, the mountaineer's ideal of garden scenery. The rock is the exciting light grey colour, is steep and appears to reach about 25 ft with the usual complement of clefts and overhangs. The hermitage, for which the house is named, is a chamber cut in the rock. Tucked away in a remote valley, 2 miles west-south-west of Mayfield, is a rock wall known as Under Rockes. This is inaccessible; it is nevertheless high and would make a worthy climbing crag. There are several more rock sites near Uckfield, all on private land and thus unavailable, while in Sheffield

---

Former stacks at Birchington. An historic picture, for vandals demolished these a decade or so ago to make way for the new promenade

Park is Gideon Mantell's 'fine lake overhung with sandstone rocks', to which we have already referred. The southern area can be summarised therefore as full of a promise, from which however climbers are largely excluded.

The idea of combining climbing with long-distance walking originated in Derbyshire where A. W. Bridge, one weekend in 1930 during the course of a twenty-one hour tramp, visited and climbed on a large number of gritstone edges. Similar marathons have since been carried out in North Wales and the Lake District. One day when no companions were available for climbing I made an expedition of this type on the Wealden sand, climbing on Bull's Hollow, the three crags at High Rocks, Eridge Green, Harrison's Rocks and Stone Farm in a trip lasting six hours—the so-called Seven Outcrops Walk. Later someone else did climbs on several other minor rocks as well in a similar but extended venture. Another possibility is a trip round all the isolated rock summits at the various crags, which have been mentioned in the foregoing.

Pinnacles and cliffs, Freshwater—Arched Rock and Stag Rock. Beyond are the magnificent chalk cliffs below Tennyson Down, leading on to Scratchells Bay and the Needles

4

COASTEERING IN THE SOUTH EAST

VERY little unspoilt scenery remains now along the coastlines of Hampshire, Sussex and Kent. Except for short stretches between Seaford and Eastbourne and in the neighbourhood of Hastings, Dover and Deal, there is almost continuous building over the whole length. Name any unsightly monstrosity, any possible misuse or commercialisation of the countryside and you will find an example here—nuclear and conventional power stations, forts and gun emplacements, the remains of wartime defences, hutments and even minefields, unlandscaped shack and bungalow towns, caravan sites, amusement parks and holiday camps, industrial developments of all kinds and so on. There would seem to be little for the climber anywhere between Bournemouth and the Thames, yet even in these unpromising circumstances something has been made, as we shall see in due course, of the great chalk cliffs of Eastbourne and the Forelands.

The walker on the shores of the Solent or Spithead would hardly regard himself as a coasteer. There are fine views across to the Isle of Wight and these seaways will always have plenty of shipping —ocean liners, naval vessels, yachts, hovercraft and so on, to maintain the interest, but it is an overpopulated scene. One can look over Buckler's Hard on the Beaulieu River, the abbey at Netley, the castle at Porchester, HMS *Victory* at Portsmouth—all of them fine examples of their kind, but concentration is necessary as the backgrounds are often alien and distracting. Selsey Bill, notably flat, leads on to Bognor, the first of a continuous chain of seaside resorts. The chalk cliffs begin 25 miles further east at Brighton, but not until 10 miles further on at Seaford do they begin to interest us.

Beyond Seaford we reach the longest stretch of unspoilt coastline in the South East. Between here and Cuckmere, Seaford Head rises imposingly and gives a foretaste of the $4\frac{1}{2}$ miles which lie ahead. From the vertical bastions of Seaford Head, complete with fort

76

and barrow, we look across at the famous Seven Sisters, where a series of dry valleys truncated by the rapid erosion of the cliffs, expose a slice of seven adjacent chalk hill ridges. The seven are called, says E. V. Lucas, Haven Brow, Short Brow, Rough Brow, Brass Point, Flagstaff Point, Bailey's Brow and West Hill Brow; a splendid walk on the characteristic springy turf leads over them from Cuckmere to Birling Gap. A staircase here sometimes gives access to the beach, sometimes not, depending on the state of erosion of the cliff. It is of course important to take a look at the state of this access before attempting a coasteering traverse along the beach from the Eastbourne direction. From Birling Gap the cliff path climbs steeply past the earthwork and ruined lighthouse at Belle Tout to something over 500 ft at Beachy Head, the highest cliff in the South East. Belle Tout lighthouse, built in 1831, was superseded in 1902 by the present lighthouse at the cliff foot; during the second world war the disused buildings were used for target practice and badly battered. Somewhere hereabouts is a man-made cave in the chalk cliff—Parson Darby's Hole. He used it, some say, as a refuge from his wife; alternatively it was a sanctuary for shipwrecked sailors. Out to sea (some 9 miles to the east) is the Royal Sovereign Lightship, soon to be replaced by a concrete tower standing on the sea bed and reaching a height of 115 ft above water level. This is being constructed near Newhaven and will in due course be towed out and sunk in position.

All along here erosion of the relatively soft rock takes place continuously and there are major changes from time to time in the contours of the cliff face. Once there were seven towers of chalk standing out from the cliff, called the Seven Charleses; the last, says Madock, fell in 1853. F. W. Bourdillon, however, recorded the survival of three of them (or the remains of three of them) to 1884; one, a mere finger of chalk, was destroyed during the construction of the new lighthouse; the second, a famous climbing pinnacle, known as the Devil's Chimney, subsided into the sea during the 1950s; only the third, Etheldreda's Pinnacle, remains and that for how long?

Edward Whymper of the Matterhorn was one of the earliest mountaineers to refer to the Head; setting out in 1860 on the first of his Alpine campaigns, he wrote:

As we steamed out into the Channel, Beachy Head came into view, and recalled a scramble of many years ago. With the impudence of ignorance, my brother and I, schoolboys both, had tried to scale that great chalk cliff. Not the head itself—where sea birds circle, and where the flints are arranged in orderly parallel lines— but at a place more to the east, where a pinnacle called the Devil's Chimney had fallen down. Since then we have been often in dangers of different kinds, but never have we more nearly broken our necks than upon that occasion.

Around the same time another Alpine climber, John Stogden, was using chalk here and elsewhere on the south coast for glissading and step-cutting. This indeed was how it was often treated in the earliest days of the sport, for the nature of the rock makes it much more suitable for the practice of Alpine techniques than for conventional rock climbing. It is soft enough to enable steps to be cut in places and certainly steep enough to require them; its disadvantages as a medium for rock climbing are the friable nature of the holds and the lack of sound belays. Neither of these would have daunted the early Alpinist and his approach to our chalk cliffs in search of practice had much the same motivation as his explorations in our home mountains. A number of well-known mountaineers were also chalk climbers and they were not afraid to describe their adventures upon it, so that by the 1890s actual routes were being recorded on the cliffs around Beachy Head. They sometimes left their ice-axes at home but they were still thinking in terms of the Alps. British mountain rock climbing however developed even faster; it offered considerably more scope, while the quality of the rock was such that difficult moves could be made under conditions where the danger was almost completely controllable. On chalk on the other hand, difficulty and danger were inseparable. The traditions which gradually grew up round British rock climbing demanded sound rock and careful safeguarding of the moving climber by a system of belaying. These requirements chalk could not fulfil, so that by about 1900 climbing had ceased altogether on Beachy Head. And it stayed that way!

It is worthwhile now to take a look at the great days of the 1890s. Charles Pilkington, writing in the Badminton Library volume on *Mountaineering*, had this to say of chalk:

 . . . the white cliffs of Old England have proved themselves too much for many of her sons. Chalk is a very troublesome material to climb; it is loose, breaks away, and if wet, either with rain or the draining of the land above, forms a sticky paste, which, lodging between the boot nails, renders them of little use. Doubtless many of those who get into difficulties are only shod for a walk on the promenade or pier, but chalk cliffs must not be treated carelessly even by the well equipped.

W. P. Haskett Smith, whose explorations in the Lake District have earned him the title of the father of British rock climbing, has plenty to say about Beachy Head in his *Rock Climbing in the British Isles – England*, which appeared in 1894. There he refers to the man who seems to have been the real pioneer.

This was Aleister Crowley, a man of peculiar and unsavoury reputation, whose biography, published a few years ago, was entitled *The Great Beast*. His only redeeming features seem to have been an interest in chess and mountaineering. As well as at Eastbourne, he climbed in British mountains, in the Alps and in the Himalaya. This is Crowley:

> The fantastic beauty of the cliffs of Beachy Head can never be understood by anyone who has not grappled with them . . . they offer rock problems as varied, interesting and picturesque as any cliffs in the world. My association with the Head possesses a charm which I have never known in any other district of England. My climbs there fulfilled all my ideas of romance, and in addition I had the particularly delightful feeling of complete originality. In other districts I could be no more than *primus inter pares*. On Beachy Head I was the only one—I had invented an entirely new branch of the sport.

His account of his actual routes on the Head was contributed by some strange quirk of choice to the *Scottish Mountaineering Club Journal*. With his friend Gregor Grant he climbed the fabulous pinnacle of the Devil's Chimney on two weekends in July 1894. (Pisgah is the main cliff behind the Chimney; Jordan was the gap between the Chimney and Pisgah; the Chimney itself comprised an inner pinnacle, the Tooth, separated by a gap, the Gash, from an outer pinnacle, the Needle.):

> 4th July, 1894. We walked along the top of the cliffs till we reached the descent to Pisgah, on which my friend fixed himself, while I descended the rotten ridge that leads to Jordan. Above and beyond rises Few Chimney, perhaps twenty feet high, affording what seemed the only possible access to the Tooth. By dint of much squirming and the judicious use of such pressure holds as were available, I succeeded in reaching the top, to find myself on the top of the block forming the eastern wall of the chimney, while the summit of the Tooth still towered above me in all its rottenness.

Both the north and the east faces were coated with loose layers of chalk, which came away with a single touch, but the east had the advantage of being less vertical. After much belabouring of it with my axe I succeeded in reducing it to a condition of comparative stability, and by dint of a few steps and hitching the rope over the top managed to struggle to the summit. The laborious nature of the climbing is evidenced by the fact that two hours and more were required to overcome a vertical height of only thirty feet. After carefully reconnnoitring the Needle, which lay beyond, and pronouncing it impossible, I rejoined my friend on Pisgah.

11th July, 1894. After lunch at the Beachy Head Hotel, we followed the usual high-level route to Pisgah, and then proceeded to do the Tooth as before, of course in much less time than on the first ascent. On this Grant 'fixed himself'—a humorous term we sometimes employ—and I went down the ridge into the Gash, 'fixed myself', and began my steps. The chalk is much firmer than on the Tooth, but the north face is, if not undercut, at least vertical, the west overhangs, and the east is about 70° if not more. On the north-east corner, therefore, three steps were cut, going as high as possible to save subsequent work. Five times I tried to cross the Gash, but with no decent handhold it is hardly to be expected that one can pull one's self up to a vertical wall. One chance, however remained. I scooped a hole out in the east face, inserted my chin and hauled. I had not shaved for a day or two, so was practically enjoying the advantages of Mummery spikes. The extra steadiness proved sufficient, and I came up into a position of the most ticklish balance conceivable, but the next step was easier, and from it I managed to hitch the rope well over. Soon I was able to get my hands on the ridge; my right leg followed, then the rest of my body, and the Needle was conquered. However, as it is not 'built for two', Grant, much to his disappointment, had to stay on the Tooth, and console himself by hoisting the Union Jack, which we left to wave triumphantly over the scene of our victory.

Etheldreda's Pinnacle nearby was also climbed:

Directly I saw this magnificent pyramid I determined to climb it at once. Two chimneys, side by side, and since named Castor and Pollux, presented the most obvious route to the ridge joining the pinnacle with the mass of the cliff. The north one (Castor) looked easy, though it was almost entirely filled with chalk dust of the consistency of fine flour, caked on the top, and having blocks of various sizes in the middle. All this, at the touch, came down, and the whole weight jammed on my legs, which were well into the chimney. A convulsive series of amoeboid movements enabled me to get out over the debris, when it immediately thundered down, leaving me in a very comfortable gap. I was soon over the jammed stone and on to the ridge. My friend refused to follow, but as he was roped I

put on a sudden pressure, and he—well—changed his mind. When
he reached the ridge I went on for the north face. This has several
natural steps, but the first two yards required a few gentle touches
with the magic wand, the chalk being very hard. Thence the route
lay westwards to the north-west corner and then back again to the
shoulder, only one step being at all awkward. The summit consists
of a big square block, which rocked and swayed under me as I sat
down upon it.

They were not always so successful, having sometimes to be
rescued:

> The Cuillin Crack is nearly 200 feet high, and affords the finest
> and most difficult piece of climbing that I have yet found in the
> whole neighbourhood. It is broken at two places, one near the
> bottom, and the other about 100 feet higher up. The first break
> presents terrible difficulty, but after incredible exertion it yielded,
> and then I got a leg and an arm jammed, and managed to wriggle
> up about sixty feet higher. At this point the rope and my strength
> were alike exhausted, some four hours, without any sort of rest,
> having already passed. Foothold and handhold there were none
> that could be relied upon to support Grant's additional weight, if
> any pressure were to be put on the rope. There was nothing for it
> but to let down a rope from above, or to descend with ignominy
> and much toil. So Grant sped away to invoke the assistance of the
> coastguard, and meanwhile I sat wedged in a most uncomfortable
> position, at the bottom of the second break, up to which I had
> struggled while waiting Grant's return. And so presently a rope was
> let down from above.

Each time on the way home they had to run the gauntlet of 'the
infidel fashion of Eastbourne and be scorned for a miller or a baker'.
   Another chalk cliff climber of the time was H. Somerset Bullock,
for many years a member of the Alpine Club, whose obituary in
the *Alpine Journal* in 1963 was contributed by a friend who had
first climbed with him on Beachy Head in 1897:

> The contrasts of the white cliffs against the blue sky above the
> immensity of the heaving channel far below was, for Bullock, an
> aesthetic shock to be numbered with Alpine memories.

From his contributions to Beachy Head literature, notably in the
Climbers' Club Journal in 1899 and the *Sussex County Magazine*
in 1935, it is clear that he had a special affection for chalk:

> . . . the face of this dizzy cliff, dazzling in the sunshine, and even
> more dangerous in mist or snow, is not for the novice, but it offers

rich rewards for the practised climber, shod with mountain boots and armed with a stout stick, if not with an ice axe. Once round the base of the first pinnacle, the most magnificent and stupendous of these chalk towers bursts upon his view. To see it to perfection, give me the dying day, when the smouldering glow of sunset fires is behind the tower, silhouetted against the thousand tints of the tapestry of the sky and sea.

And there, a year before the end of the last century, the recorded story ends. Thenceforward, while British mountain rock climbing continued to expand broadly, only a handful of climbers has looked at our chalk cliffs.

We have seen how chalk rated a mention in the Badminton Library volume on *Mountaineering* in 1892. The next textbook reference, which occurred in 1920 in Geoffrey Winthrop Young's *Mountain Craft*, serves to emphasise the lack of progress in the twentieth century:

> Chalk, and the methods of dealing with it, form a study by themselves. Chalk climbing provides the missing link between rock and ice technique. Those who frequent its cliffs use big claws and ice methods, and pronounce it to be an unrivalled training for ice work. Its occasional hard surface and its abundant projecting flints, whose security is in inverse ratio to their graspability, have to be treated with the measures of precaution proper to unsound rock.

The Lonsdale Library volume on *Mountaineering* (c. 1936), where the relevant pages were contributed by that redoubtable veteran Haskett Smith, is confined to what happened before 1900. It was at about this time, however, that the first chinks began to appear in the 'sound rock' basis of British rock climbing. Certain crags in Wales, like the Devil's Kitchen cliff for example, of rock not entirely faultless and having more than the usual quota of vegetation, were attacked by that great innovator J. Menlove Edwards. The same movement spread also to the Lake District. Then after the second world war limestone, once the preserve of a few eccentric enthusiasts, swept into favour. Poor quality rock is accepted now as part of the hazard of modern climbing and this might well lead on to chalk climbing once again, now the logical final stage of the development of British mountain rock climbing instead of the sideline development of Alpine mountaineering that it used to be. In France, as we shall see in due course, chalk cliffs are climbed on the coast near Étretat and at a number of places in the Seine valley.

This French variety is firm enough for pitons and the climbing is of high standard, with some artificial. It seems probable that their material is sounder because the bedding is nearly horizontal, while on Beachy Head and elsewhere here the beds are sloping and the crags subside at intervals into the sea. Anyone interested should look around in this country for horizontally-bedded chalk and there indeed they should also find climbing potential.

An expert who has climbed on Beachy Head within the last decade describes the climbing as falling into two categories— bouldering on the lowest 30 ft (chiefly on the Head itself for a mile or so east of the lighthouse and on the Seven Sisters just east of Cuckmere Haven) and occasionally mountaineering-type climbing for the whole height of the cliff, needing ice axes and step cutting. 'I have sometimes wondered', he adds, 'if Beachy Head isn't the cliff of the future'.

For the present the tendency towards chalk is counteracted to some extent by the modern improvements in transport, which have brought much more desirable rock types within reach. Climbers who twenty years ago might have gone to Eastbourne now go to Swanage where the rock is so much more reliable. The sheer novelty of these great white crags still attracts the occasional climber. Maybe he treats it as rock climbing, maybe as practice for Alpine mountaineering, or maybe merely tests himself as suggested by Frank Smythe:

> Anyone who can gaze unmoved upon the sea from the edge of Beachy Head need have no qualms as to his reactions upon the most sensational of Alpine precipices.

The Head offers one further prospect to the coasteer—a sea-level traverse of nearly 4 miles round the foot from Eastbourne to Birling Gap. Richard Jefferies, one of the first to tramp this beach, describes a familiar sensation of the coasteer:

> The sea seems higher than the spot where I stand, its surface on on a higher level—raised like a green mound—as if it could burst in and occupy the space up to the foot of the cliff in a moment.

There are none of the more difficult coasteering problems here— curtains of rock, absence of beach, and so on, which enliven similar passages in places like North Devon. One would need to check the tide times carefully, look out for rock falls and make sure beforehand that the exits were still operational, otherwise the 4 miles to Birling Gap might become another $2\frac{1}{2}$ on to Cuckmere. Just beyond the end of Eastbourne front is a little pinnacle, the Sugar Loaf, which gives a climb of difficult standard up the ridge facing the sea.

The coast on the far side of Eastbourne, corresponding now to the low-lying clay lands of the Weald, is flat across Pevensey Levels —a place for invasions. Here, where William the Conqueror stumbled on landing and passed it off with a laugh, we see the relics of Anderida (a Roman fort of the Saxon Shore), of a Norman castle inside the Roman perimeter and of some Martello towers, built years later anti-Buonaparte. Further on rise sandstone cliffs corresponding to the Wealden Sandstone.

They are unpretentious at first being mixed up with the houses fronting the sea at Bexhill and St Leonard's. At one time there was a pinnacle in the sandstone at Galley Hill. Considerable changes have taken place on the coastline at Hastings during historical times. Formerly the sea beat against the crags on West Hill, which is topped by the fragmentary ruins of Hastings Castle. After half of it had been eroded away, the growth of a shingle bank protected the remainder; later, as the sea receded even further, buildings were erected below these ancient cliffs. This is the first extensive exposure of rock, and climbs are said to have been done; the walls west and south of the castle are unlikely because of the public nature of the place and the poor quality and steepness of the upper part. However the broken sandy crag somewhat further east may give a climb or two, while there is some scrambling also for the 'nurse escaping feet' of very young aspirants. The castle above, a magnificent viewpoint, has an impressive dungeon hewn from solid rock. In the valley to the east St Clement's show caves covering an area of three acres are of unknown antiquity, probably underground workings for sand.

Beyond lies East Hill flanked by a fine expanse of massive sandstone, by far the most impressive outcrop of Wealden Sand anywhere. Unfortunately there are emphatic snags for the climber. True the vertical walls are cracked and fissured and would appear to offer routes, but the boulders strewn at the foot betoken an unacceptable amount of rock fall, while a very steep earth/rock mixture leads on from the crags to the cliff top. Hastings Town Council bans access to the summit with a substantial fence and frequent notice boards indicate the folly of crossing it. Though one hears rumours of an occasional attempt, there is in fact no written record of a climb anywhere hereabouts. It is possible that the diligent searcher might find one, just as has been done in similar terrain in the environs of Bude, for example. One of the features of this east Cornwall coastline is the small number of routes available compared with the large amount of rock exposed; similarly here at Hastings these rocks which look largely unpromising might yield a line or two where the many obvious dangers were absent for one reason or another. However the public nature of the place, its comparatively small scale and the extreme rottenness of the rock make it inadvisable to try. The litter of boulders at the cliff foot seems also to preclude the possibility of a coasteering traverse, but in fact a safe way can be found at a low enough state of the tide; at least there are no obstacles of the type which make similar expeditions so sporting in other parts of the land. The existence of an exit on ahead must of course be verified beforehand.

Travelling more comfortably along the clifftop we come in half a mile to Ecclesbourne Glen, where the sea is, as often, cutting back the cliff line faster than the small stream in the valley can cut it down. This process produces the inevitable coast waterfall and periodic interruption of access to the beach. The sandstone is exposed on either hand but never unfortunately in a climbable form. Over the next hill is Fairlight Glen with a number of small rock outcrops, including the well-known Lovers' Seat, which offer a short climb or two. Fairlight Down (550 + ft) above is the last hill of the southerly branch of the Forest Ridge, which has been continuous for some 20 miles from Cross-in-Hand south of Mayfield. The view, says Lower's *History of Sussex* quoted by Topley, embraces 'ten towns, sixty-six churches, five castles, forty windmills and seventy Martello towers'. Also further off, adds Topley are 'the dark cliffs of Boulogne and the chalk cliffs north of it'. C. G. Harper has given an account of the Martello towers. Altogether seventy-six of them were built along the south coast in the early years of the nineteenth century. They cost between £10,000 and £20,000 each and have walls 9 ft thick on the seaward side and 6 ft thick on the landward. The base was the magazine, with two living rooms above; the guns were on the roof behind a 4 ft parapet. In the early years of the present century many were let as holiday cottages at rents of £4 to £5 per annum.

The new town, or village, of Fairlight, though pleasant maybe for those that live there, is only an obstruction to the coastal traveller. Beyond at Cliff End lies another interesting stretch of rocky cliff 60 ft high, where the sandstone outcrops remind us once again of the inland climbing rocks. There may be a few routes on the lower tier but the horizontal strata above look woefully rotten, while the upper tier is capped by loose slopes and thick vegetation. Soon the cliff line begins to swing inland where the flat triangular promontory of Dungeness, comprising the Marshes of Romney, Walland, Guildeford and Denge, now separates it from the sea's edge. At Pett Level there is a sandstone outcrop called Toot Rock, on which routes are said to have been made, though it is rather mixed up with the houses. The surroundings are depressingly strewn with shacks and bungalows. Parts are below sea level and only a massive wall keeps the sea at bay. During World War II this area was deliberately flooded as a defence measure and, while thus deserted, became an extremely interesting wild life sanctuary.

The original cliffline extends behind the Marsh for more than 20 miles and does not reach the present coastline again until beyond Hythe. It would make an interesting walk and is certainly an alternative for the coasteer who might find himself less attracted to the shingle banks, the beaches and the atomic power station of Dungeness itself. At its foot runs the Royal Military Canal which was built for coastal defence during the Napoleonic wars, contemporary with the Martello towers. Its military origins can be clearly discerned in an aerial view which emphasises the regular system of right-angled bends with each section enfilading the next. Two miles beyond Pett Level is Winchelsea, a former Cinque Port now deserted by the sea; gateways to the old walled town remain. Nearer the sea but cut off in its turn is Camber Castle, a Henry VIII coastal defence fort, now surrounded by grassy flats, dunes and shingle banks. Most of Dungeness is flint, but some pebbles have come from as far away as Budleigh Salterton:

> The loose shingle comprising this vast waste of Dungeness is some eight or nine feet deep, and most difficult and exhausting to walk upon. Indeed, the only way to progress for any distance upon it is by wearing upon the feet the contrivances called 'backstays', which are simply boards five inches wide and some nine or ten inches long. They serve exactly the purpose fulfilled by snow-shoes, and prevent or stay one from slipping back. . . . They are fastened

either by straps over the boots, or are worn on the naked feet by passing the straps over the instep and round the big toe.

This was Harper fifty years ago!

The eastern side of the Marsh shelters behind the protecting Dymchurch Wall, 4 miles long and 20 ft high. A strange effect is experienced hereabouts, says the guidebook, in motoring or walking about the Marsh at high tide, 'for the sea appears to be, and indeed is, higher than one's head'. On the slopes of the now rapidly converging cliffline are the ancient walls of Stutfall Castle, the outlines of which have been partially obliterated by landslides. It was a ruin even in Leland's time (sixteenth century):

> There remayneth at this day the ruines of a stronge fortresse of the Britons hangging on the hil, and cummying down to the very fote. The cumpase of the forteresse semeth to be a X acres, and be lykelyhood yt had sum walle beside that strecchid up to the very top of the hille . . . the old walles made of Britons' brikes, very large and great flynt set together almost indissolubely with morters made of smaule pybble.

The Lower Greensand outcrops at the coast between Hythe and Folkestone form massive sandstone cliffs in places and east of Folkestone Gault Clay is exposed on the foreshore. The chalk cliffs and the Upper Greensand resting on the clay provide the classical situation for landslips, which are prominent in the Warren area between here and Dover.

'From Folkstone', says Camden, 'the chalky rocks as it were hanging one by another, run in a continued ridge for five miles altogether, as far as Dover'. The Warren, sometimes called Little Switzerland, which stretches for nearly 2 miles to Abbot's Cliff, is a chaos of small hills and valleys between the beach and the line of the chalk cliffs behind. It is traversed by the main line railway and by paths. There are interesting plants, fossils and smugglers' caves. The coasteer can pass this way and over Abbot's Cliff and Shakespeare Cliff (both around 500 ft) to reach Dover in 5 miles; it is also possible to travel the whole way on the foreshore at low tide. However, this is not an unspoilt countryside. Borings for the Channel Tunnel were made here as long ago as the 1880s; there was a colliery alongside Shakespeare Cliff abandoned in the same period; the railway obtrudes almost the whole way, and one is always liable to stumble across parts of the defences of Dover.

Shakespeare Cliff, which buttresses Dover on the west side, and is thus one of the 'white cliffs', is named for its mention in *King Lear*. We read there of an early cliff climber with utilitarian motives:

> . . . half way down
> Hangs one that gathers samphire—dreadful trade.

This is a rock plant, the leaves of which were pickled and used in salads or as a sauce for meat. The technique was described in the *Guide to Watering Places*:

> The poor people who gather it fix a rope to an iron crow driven in the ground at the top of the cliff, then descending by its aid over the precipice, in a basket gather the samphire; an employment which makes the spectator shudder.

A climber on the cliff would do much the same and have much the same effect on the present-day onlooker.

The harbour at Dover is entirely artificial. The town has had a famous history, among the relics of which are a Roman lighthouse and a splendid castle, as well as more modern defence forts. Now it is the English climber's gateway to the mountains of Europe. The 2 miles of cliff between here and the South Foreland, the other half of the 'white cliffs', are close on 400 ft high. There is a cliff path, but with the same used-and-left-derelict appearance which we found on the Folkestone side. On the South Foreland is a lighthouse which looks across 20 miles of Channel to another on Cap Gris Nez and to the chalk of Cap Blanc Nez which has been used by climbers. Here is a turning point in the coast, which now runs due north; a mile away is St Margaret's Bay and beyond it the cliffs continue, losing height steadily now, until they disappear finally at Kingsdown.

Offshore the natural anchorage called the Downs is sheltered by the Goodwin Sands, exposed at low water, said to be the remains of the island of Loomea destroyed by storms in 1099. Parties land occasionally. Lighthouse construction having proved impossible, the danger area for shipping is marked by a series of lightships—North Goodwin, South Goodwin, South Sand, East Goodwin and Varne, well seen from the cliffs by St Margaret's Bay. With the lighthouses at South Foreland, North Foreland and Cap Gris Nez, this adds up to a well-lit corner of the oceans.

Some 9 miles of flat coastline follow past Walmer, Deal and

Sandwich, all with Henry VIII coastal defence castles. Such is the configuration of the final reaches of the Stour that the coastwise traveller must go inland to Sandwich in order to cross the river. Here he is on the brink of the former Wantsum Channel which used to separate the Isle of Thanet from the mainland and was defended by Roman forts at Richborough close at hand and at Reculver on the northern coast. Richborough is a fine ruin, of which Leland wrote:

> The mayn se ys now off of yt a myle by reason of wose, that hath there swollenup. The site of the old town or castel ys wonderful faire upon an hille. The walles the wich remayn ther yet be in cumpase almost as much as the Tower of London. They have bene very hye, thykke, stronge and wel embateled. The mater of them is flynt, mervelous and long brykes both white and redde after the Britons fascion.

Thanet, not quite reaching 200 ft at its highest point, is ringed by chalk cliffs more or less hidden by a continuous line of resorts—Ramsgate, Broadstairs, Margate and Westgate. It is not coasteering country, as Harper says of it:

> They are not cliffs on the heroic scale, these chalky bastions. They run from Ramsgate to Birchington with a toy-like, artificial effect; rather, you know, as if some enterprising Earl's Court exhibition syndicate had erected them. They are strangely unconvincing to those who have been used to the great red cliffs of Devon, or the mighty granite heights of Cornwall. Being of no great height, and of such unpicturesque outline, and having been so railed in and scraped and tunnelled and mended with brick, and in all manner of ways impertinently interferred with, they look like the products of art, and a very poor art too.

A shell grotto at Margate, approached by a 60 ft passage, claimed as a temple, a Viking catacomb and so forth, dates in fact from the early nineteenth century. There are caves at Botany Bay and Kingsgate, where the so-called Smugglers' Cave is 280 ft long and a natural formation. The fine chalk stacks which used to grace the cliffs by Birchington have been blasted to make way for the new promenade—but promenades are so common and chalk stacks so rare! Now only one slight pinnacle of 20 ft or so remains.

Climbing on these chalk cliffs from Folkestone round to Thanet also has its history. During the last century one very famous climber was associated with this coastline—no less than A. F. Mummery—who lived at Dover. He contributed the notes on chalk to W. P.

Haskett Smith's *Rock Climbing in the British Isles – England*, the first-ever guidebook to British rocks. Mummery's views on chalk were much the same as ours today:

> Though this can hardly be regarded as a good rock for climbing, much excellent practice can be gained on it. As a general rule, it is only sufficiently solid for real climbing for the first twenty feet above high water mark, though here and there forty feet of fairly trustworthy rock may be found. These sections of hard chalk are invariably those which at their base are washed by the sea at high tide; all others are soft and crumbly. . . . Chalk, it must be remembered, is extremely rotten and treacherous, very considerable masses coming away occasionally with a comparatively slight pull. In any place where a slip is not desirable, it is unwise to depend exclusively on a single hold, as even the hardest and firmest knobs, that have stood the test of years, give way suddenly without any apparent reason. The flints imbedded in the chalk are similarly untrustworthy; in fact, if they project more than an inch or so, they are, as a rule, insecure. The surface of the chalk is smooth and slimy if wet, dusty if dry, and does not afford the excellent hold obtained on granite. As a whole it may be regarded as a treacherous and difficult medium, and one which is likely to lead those practising on it to be very careful climbers.

Of the nature of the climbing he wrote:

> Whilst any considerable ascent, other than up the extremely steep slopes of grass which sometimes clothes the gullies and faces, is out of the question, traverses of great interest and no slight difficulty are frequently possible for considerable distances.

This brought him into conflict with the monstrous Crowley, who held exactly the opposite view—his climbs were not low-level

———

The Needles, showing lighthouse and pinnacles. On the right is Scratchells Bay; on the left, steep chalk cliffs lead on to the facing multi-coloured sands of Alum Bay. The chalk backbone of the island trends away to the right into the distance

traverses but vertical face climbs and pinnacles. Crowley wrote to Mummery, who, says Crowley:

> . . . wrote back rather superciliously to the effect that there were certainly grassy gullies which corresponded to my description, but they were not what he called climbing. I replied, thanking him and begging him to accept a few photographs of the grassy gullies under discussion. These showed the most formidable-looking pinnacles in the British Isles, and vertical cracks as precipitous as anything in Cumberland. He wrote back immediately a warm letter of congratulation. It was evident that we had been using the word 'chalk' to cover two widely different species of material.

A modern climber who has experimented with ascents on chalk cliffs during the last twenty years is R. H. A. Staniforth of Broadstairs. He has approached chalk with traditional rock climbing tactics considerably modified but not so far with the elaborate security methods which the French are using at Étretat and at Cap Blanc Nez. His views on the medium are thus very similar to Mummery's, even though the routes nowadays go up and over the top rather than hugging the lower 30 ft of sea-scoured rock. Staniforth writes:

> Chalk climbing calls for more expertise than is usually applied to conventional crags; intending aspirants should put in as much practice as possible in chalk quarries beforehand. Owing to the friable nature of the stuff it can be more than normally risky for experts and could be suicidal for novices. When dry it is apt to crumble, when wet from either rain, mist, dew or damp sea atmosphere, as it so often is along the Channel coast, there is nothing more treacherous. Precautionary top ropes and extra life-lines are essential to safety at all times. Any approach to it calls for the utmost respect and precaution.

The Cathedral, Salisbury. The famous 400 ft spire, scene of legendary ascents by tipsy gallants at the Ancient Fair and of armchair explorations of a later age

F

Mummery had made numerous climbs on the cliffs between Folkestone and Dover, where, he said:

> . . . a great amount of climbing on grass and crumbly chalk slopes can be obtained; almost every gully and face can be ascended from the sea, or the S.E. Railway, to the top. It is necessary to remember that in dry weather the grass and the earth which underlies it is of the consistency of sand, and great care is a requisite; after rain the grass is of course slippery; but the underlying material adheres more firmly to the cliff. It is unnecessary to add that a slip on any of these slopes would almost certainly prove fatal. On the face of Abbot's Cliff and to the westward some traverses may be effected at a height of 200 feet or more above the base; they do not, however, compare for climbing with the traverses on the other side of Dover. As one goes westwards, the angle of the cliffs becomes less, and from Abbot's Cliff towards Folkestone it is rarely necessary to use one's hands, though very nice 'balance' is essential, as the results of a slip would usually be serious. Above the Warren, still nearer Folkestone, the slopes become easy, and after heavy snow afford excellent glissades.

Staniforth describes more recent experience:

> West of Dover, the fine twins of Shakespeare and Abbot's Cliffs present difficult problems. Climbing hereabouts is exposed and could rightly be classed as extremely severe and decidedly dangerous. After several abortive assaults I managed them both some time ago but success was due to my team support; both cliffs and risks are far too high for unassisted stunts. There is a so-called easy route up the Abbot, which I have safely traversed up and down solo, using self belays and safety line in lieu of top rope. The way goes via the Rotunda and Hanging Face caves near the summit, both of which give convenient bivouacs. Further west the Folkestone Warren offers numerous faces with ample scope for using outsize pitons, small axe and, when damp and slimy, crampons. These should have dull rather than sharp points; I have in fact successfully used a home-made pair with screw-in pyramid soccer studs. Several of the faces in the Warren have fallen to us as a team, while two I have done solo. . . .

Mummery's low-level traverses, to which we have already referred, are on the cliffs to the east of Dover and are perhaps the earliest examples of this outstanding feature of coasteering. His aim was to work out a route to various small beaches cut off from the outer world by high tide and cliffs; nowadays there are many miles of this sort of thing in the West Country. Mummery, one of the greatest rock climbers of his age, wrote of the practice value of chalk climbing on the lower stretches of these cliffs:

. . . scrambles of every variety of difficulty may be found, some being amongst the hardest *mauvais pas* with which I am acquainted. Owing to the proximity of the ground, they afford the climber an excellent opportunity of ascertaining the upper limit of his powers. Such knowledge is a possession of extreme value, yet in most other places it is indesirable to ascertain it too closely.

Staniforth notes the St Margaret's Bay area as offering 'plenty of scope to the adventurous climber with sheer ascents, clefts, cracks and traverses in abundance'. All attractive, but none to be considered at all safe.

If any climbs are to be found on Thanet, and some certainly have been done, they are likely to be too public to be worthwhile, except at unorthodox hours or seasons. The stacks at Birchington, formerly accessible by 'Tyrolean' traverse (using the climbing rope as a bridge) are now, alas, debris on the seabed.

Leaving Thanet we can continue to walk along the coast for a time, though when coasteering ceases and its estuary or riverbank analogue begins, is largely a matter of definition. Reculver at the northern end of the Wantsum Channel was the site of a Roman fort; the twin towers of the ruined Saxon church have long been preserved as a seamark. The changing nature of the coastline is emphasised by air pictures taken in 1948 and 1961, which are printed side by side in *The English Coast* by J. A. Steers. The first shows empty fields round the fort and towers; the second has these same fields filled with row upon row of caravans, several hundreds of them.

On ahead it is all very flat. After Herne Bay and Whitstable we come to a series of islands around the mouth of the Medway, of which the largest is Sheppey. Here at Warden Point, where the land is sliding slowly into the sea, pyritised fossils and plants are found on the beach. Of this 'Land's End of Sheppey' Geoffrey Grigson has written:

> There was never such a natural rubbish heap, such a jumble of earth and clay, such a cracking and flowing, such mud, such instability. Picturesque, no doubt; full of greys and browns and rich ochres and umbers, all shaped in ups and downs, and ledges, and lava-like mud-flows and tumbles, right to the sea. And if the tide is out, down below, your taste for peculiar places, your connoisseurship, may now be shaken a little by the wide extent of grey mud (as it looks) and by the muddy rippling of the sea beyond it.

On the far side of the Medway is the Isle of Grain dominated by a huge oil refinery; the Thames between here and Southend is some 4 miles wide. It narrows rapidly and soon only 1½ miles separate the Cooling Marshes here from Canvey Island over yonder. Cooling has a fine castle gatehouse, while in the graveyard of its tiny church Pip met the dreadful Magwitch in the early pages of *Great Expectations*:

> . . . the dark flat wilderness beyond the churchyard, intersected with dykes and mounds and gates, with scattered cattle feeding on it, was the marshes; and the low leaden line beyond was the river; and the distant savage lair from which the wind was rushing was the sea. . . .

Inland a few miles at Strood by Rochester there is a site of interest to cavers. When excavations for the city waterworks were made in 1879 a natural cave was discovered in the chalk. Work and natural water flow in the ensuing years culminated in 1913, when 160 ft of passage was exposed. Though possibly still in existence all this is inaccessible at the present time.

The last of the cliffy coastlines is at Thanet and thenceforward through north Kent, Essex and most of Suffolk the margin of the sea is flat, the very antithesis of mountain country. In East Anglia, says Andrew Young, 'the only hills are snowy mountains lent by the sky and piled up on the wide horizons'. Only in places has East Anglia suffered the fate of Sussex, the coastline of which is nothing more than a continuous line of towns and houses. Here, in contrast, travel along the coast is often made difficult by deeply penetrating estuaries, marshes and drainage channels and it is frequently necessary to turn inland to look for bridges. The coasteer might add a collapsible boat to his equipment and take to the sea from time to time in order to follow his chosen way. His route will follow sea walls between flat land on the one side and flat sea on the other, joined over his head by a colossal arch of sky. He may well notice in passing the mysterious 'Red Hills of Essex', used from ancient times until 150 years ago to obtain salt from sea water by pouring it over red hot bars. Up to three acres of land were enclosed by a bank, all brick red in colour, with a ditch around for the water supply.

On this wide coast south of the estuary of the Blackwater stood the Roman fort of Othona. Very little of it remains, though astride one wall is the tiny Saxon chapel of St Peter-on-the-Wall, built from some of the original stones. The Roman road to it from Bradwell-on-Sea is only a trackway; and Grigson says of it:

> The track keeps it free of cars and unviolated, but the sea does not lap wall or bastion, as at Porchester, for example; at ordinary tide it does not lap even the shore, keeping its distance across the saltings. Yet everything combines, landscape, seascape, extent and detail, civilisation, a past and a surrounding present always suggestive, and wonderful enough in most conditions from snow to sunlight.

It is left to our generation to spoil it all with a huge power station only 2 miles away, so that in future one must start here and walk southwards with never a backward glance.

At the Stour-Orwell estuary we pass from Essex into Suffolk but the flat coastline and the vast sky remain with us. The huge shingle spit of Orford Ness, which deflects the Alde River from Aldeburgh to North Weir Point off Shingle Street 11 miles to the south, is one of the geomorphological wonders of England. There is another great power station at Sizewell beyond Aldeburgh; then a few miles further north we reach Dunwich, a celebrated erosion site, where a medieval city and port were submerged by the sea, 'moving for ever, like a ruminating beast, insatiable, indefatigable'. Geoffrey Grigson describes this typical Suffolk scenery:

> Yet upon its own account, how fantastic a sweep of land and water! A sweep of grey water, a sweep of chocolate shingle; a curve where the cliffs give out, mile after mile, away to Walberswick and Southwold. Landward, a huge low extent of marshes and commons distinctly marked with church towers. Seaward, how extraordinary a grey! And this whole affair, sea and shingle and land, laid across the world, underneath how enormous, how important a sky!

This eroded coastline continues all the way to Norfolk.

5

SOLENT SHORES

THE Isle of Wight, 'in shape somewhat resembling a bird with expanded wings', lies athwart the mouth of Southampton Water separated from the mainland by the famous channels of Solent to the west and Spithead to the east. The name is said to be derived from Ynys yr Wyth—Isle of the Channel. It is in fact the former south wall of the valley of the Solent River which continued the line of the present River Frome to a mouth somewhere east of Spithead. The facing strata of the Dorset coast round Swanage were part of this same south wall, the chalk ridge of the Purbeck Hills and Old Harry being continuous at one time with the corresponding rocks of the Needles and Tennyson Down on the Island. From a comparison between the cross sections of the river valleys of Wight and the areas which they drain at present it can be deduced that this wall once extended considerably to the south. But under constant wave attack the coastline moved gradually northwards until a change in the relative levels of sea and land finally breached the wall and the sea flooded into the Solent Valley separating Wight from the mainland.

Along the coastline of around 60 miles there are some stretches comparatively unspoilt, where walking is still a delight. In fact there is more here for the coast walker than in the counties of Kent, Sussex and Hampshire put together. The island as a whole is an epitome of south-east English scenery. The chalk backbone reaching from the Needles promontory to Culver Cliff by Sandown is a typical piece of downland rising to 702 ft at Brighstone Down. In the south between St Catherine's and Shanklin a second chalk mass reaches 785 ft at St Boniface Down, the highest point of the island. The land between these two chalk ridges has much in common with the Weald, the Greensands, Gault Clay and Wealden Clay and Sands outcropping in the same sequence and being exposed where the sea has cut across the strata along the south-westerly coastline and again between Culver Cliff and Bonchurch. This too is a denuded dome for the rivers which formerly drained it have cut down through the main chalk ridge, just as we saw in the case of the North and South Downs and the Wealden dome. Thus the Rivers Medina, East Yar and West Yar all rise near the south coast and flow through gaps in the chalk, with Newport, Brading and Freshwater gap settlements comparable with Dorking, Maidstone etc. To the north of the main chalk ridge we find strata of more recent rocks similar, as might be expected, to those of the Hampshire Basin on the other side of the water. The varied inland scenery of this range of rock types and their exposure one after the other on the coastline make the island an attractive place for geologists. Fossils are plentiful, notably at Compton Chine, in some of the beds at Alum Bay, on Headon and Hamstead Hills and at Colwell Bay. There is a museum of Isle of Wight geology in the Public Library at Sandown.

The so-called Undercliff between Bonchurch and Niton is of particular interest to the student of landscape. Here, as in the Warren at Folkestone and in the Lyme Regis/Seaton area on the borders of Dorset and Devon, strata of comparatively hard rock rest on outward sloping bands of clay, and landslips have occasionally occurred. A cliffline of the hard rock some distance inland looks out over a plain as at St Lawrence or over an area of broken ground as at Bonchurch, to the sea sometimes as much as half a mile away. These exceptionally well-sheltered places have a very pleasant micro-climate. The chines are another interesting feature of the island scenery. These are deep narrow valleys running down to the sea, cut in soft strata by comparatively small streams with small catchment areas, making interesting breaks in the coastline and often carrying prolific vegetation.

The hill walk along the main chalk ridge begins above the Needles promontory—the jutting western prow of the Island. A century and a half ago the scene could be described in these words:

> On one of the highest of these eminences is a signal station and on another a lighthouse. From the last which is near the extremity of the island, the spectator has a view of the bold, rocky semi-circular hollow, six hundred feet high, known by the appellation of St Christopher's Cliff, with the Needle Rocks below, which, since the fall of the most slender and lofty one about forty years ago, appear more like wedges set on their bases, or the ragged grinders of an enormous jaw, than the instrument from which they receive their name.

Now in these days of scenic appreciation and awareness all this is barred to us for HM Government combines with the British Aircraft Corporation to exclude us from the finest part. Coastguards occupying the old fort on the clifftop bar us from gazing down (or perhaps, who knows? climbing down) the fine chalk arête which runs down towards the pinnacles and the lighthouse. The British Aircraft Corporation permits a distant view of the pinnacles through a barbed-wire fence at a range of not far short of half a mile, but there seems no prospect whatsoever of looking down into the magnificent recesses of Scratchell's Bay. Turning our backs upon these manifestations of modern technology, we come soon to a summit of 462 ft, steep slopes leading down to vertical chalk walls on either hand, with to the north a glimpse of the variegated colours of Alum Bay.

Another 1½ miles of upland walking leads to Tennyson Down, presented to the National Trust in 1927 in memory of the poet who lived and worked for many years at Freshwater. The cross of Cornish granite is 38 ft high. The eastern slopes of the Down lead on to Freshwater Bay and a gap so close to sea level that this small piece of Wight only just escapes being an island of its own. On the far side the ridge rises quickly again with steep slopes and vertical cliffs on the south side. After a mile the Wealden beds begin to come in at Compton Chine, the coastline slants away to the south-east while the chalk ridge runs straight ahead inland. It is National Trust again, reaching 538 ft at Five Barrows, a Bronze Age cemetery north of Brook.

Just off the ridge on the south side beyond the Brook-Shalcombe road is the Longstone, a 14 ft monolith of iron sandstone from the

---

Page 101

The White Horse, Uffington, with the castle. The great hollow of the Manger, into which the lads chased the bounding cartwheel, is picked out by shadows below the carved figure. On the left of the Manger is the hill where St George slew the dragon

Page 102

(*left*) Bridge climbing near Oxford—a disused railway bridge at Kidlington; (*right*) climbers at Étretat in action on the chalk cliffs of the Manneport

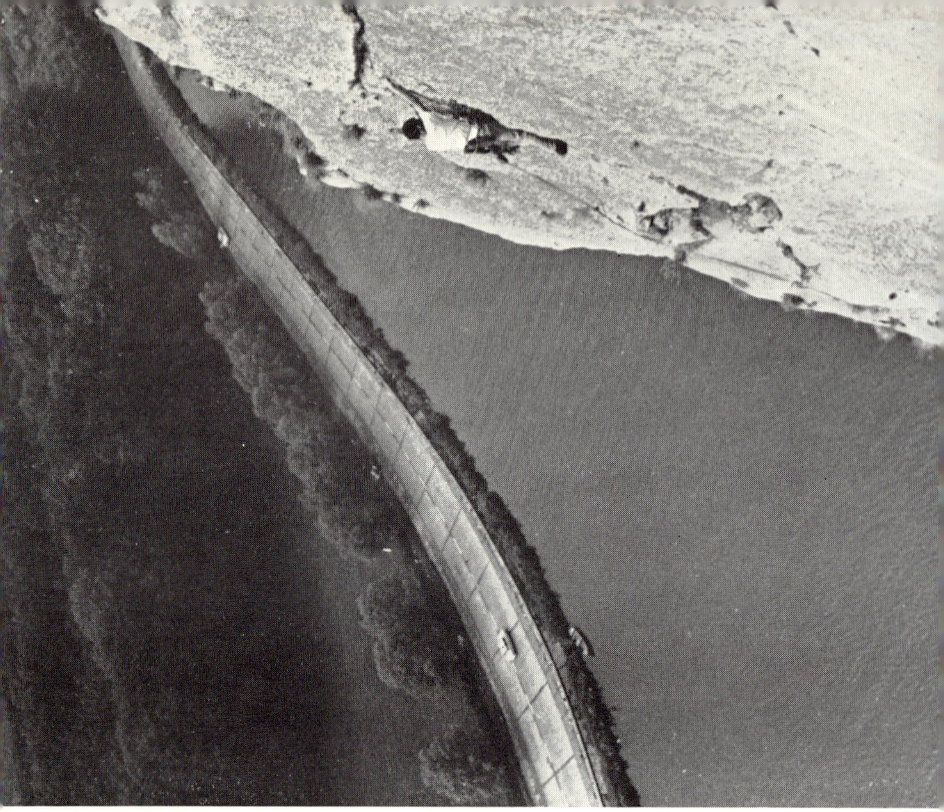

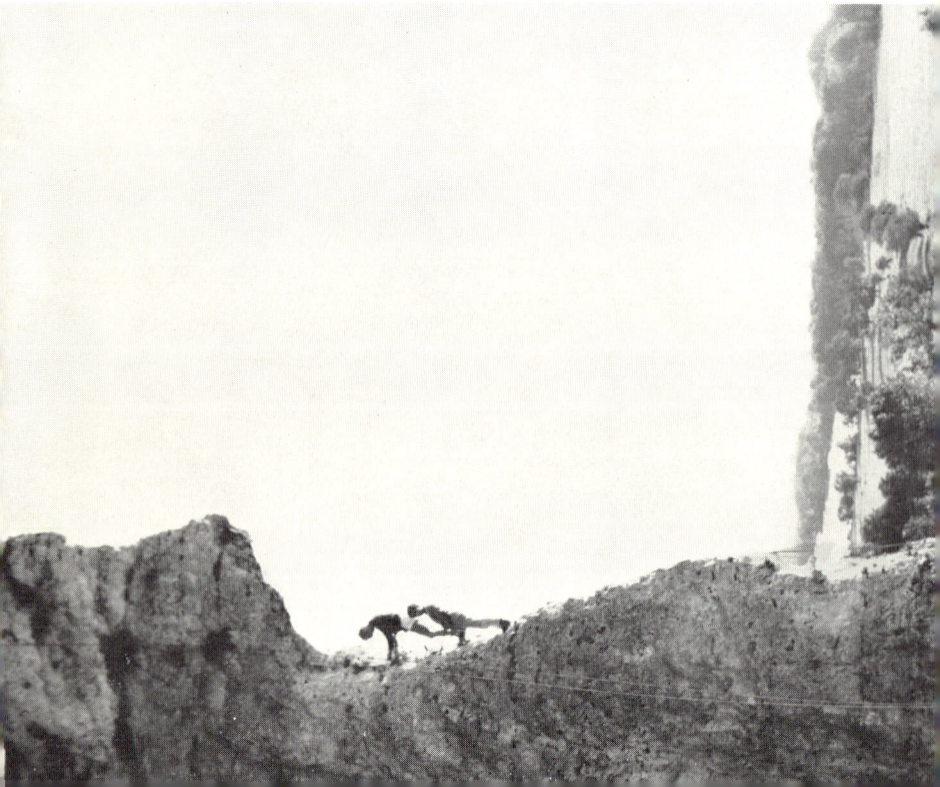

Lower Greensand, all that remains of a long barrow. There is a well-preserved sixteenth-century manor house at Mottistone at the foot of the hill. The scarp slope of the main ridge is on the south side here and the hill summits are often covered by woods. In less than 2 miles we reach Brighstone Down (702 ft) the highest point of the range. The considerable town of Newport, reached over Idlecombe and Bowcombe Downs, occupies the next prominent gap; almost a suburb is Carisbrooke with the ruins of a shell-keep type castle where King Charles I was imprisoned for a period. There is a museum of relics from this and other incidents in its history; an ingenious lifting mechanism operated by a donkey raises buckets of water from the deep castle well for the entertainment of tourists.

The hills soon reach over 400 ft again at Arreton Down, the way often shared with the motorised climber who here sees as much of the view as the traveller on foot. In a situation such as this Celia Fiennes noted, even as we do, that:

. . . upon most of the high hills you see the wall of the sea on both sides, if not all around you as in some places. . . .

After crossing Ashley Down with its daymark and Brading Down to the East Yar at Brading, thenceforward the remainder of the hill line is short but outstanding. Bembridge and Culver Downs culminate in the great chalk headland of Culver Cliff, with fine views up and down the coast and across the waterways leading to Portsmouth and Southampton. By this route the total distance from end to end of the Island is around 22 miles.

The other chalk mass, considerably less extensive, begins at St Catherine's Hill above St Catherine's Point. The former lighthouse

---

Page 103

Cliff climbing at Swanage. The climb is the Traverse of the Gods. This is the pendulum movement near the start where the climber, here Peter Gillman, swings on the rope across an impassable cleft. Note that this too is a spectator area

Page 104

(*left*) Climbing in the Seine Valley, typical of the chalk faces between Mantes and Rouen, which are extensively climbed; (*right*) climbing above the River Meuse. The very popular limestone crags at Freyr in the Ardennes, which rise straight from the waters of the river

on the hilltop dates back to the fourteenth century; the modern lighthouse (1840) is placed as usual at a much lower level on the undercliff where, though the range is less, the light is less often obscured by cloud. On a spur to the north is the Alexandrian Pillar (or Hoy's Monument), 70 ft high, which commemorates the visit of Alexander I of Russia in 1814; it carries additionally a plaque relating to the Crimea War. The River Medina, which reaches the sea at Cowes in the north, rises hereabouts.

Beyond Niton the walker proceeds along the edge above the Undercliff by St Lawrence to Ventnor. A short distance back from the edge the hills are somewhat higher—Week Down is 690 ft and a ridge running northwards from here reaches 741 ft above Appuldurcombe House. The steep slopes of St Boniface Down rise immediately above Ventnor. The summit of 785 ft is occupied by a wireless station and access to the highest point is denied to the walker, as well as to the motorist who reaches this point by the well-maintained access road. These buildings and masts associated with Air Traffic Control, which completely ruin the Down as a viewpoint, could readily be sited elsewhere since a long-distance visual path across the sea can hardly be essential to their function. Many such sites, willingly given up for our defence in times of war, have been retained far too long for a continuing peacetime function, so that now many years afterwards it seems unlikely that they will ever revert to us, as of course they most certainly should.

The ridge runs on to Shanklin Down (773 ft) with a view over Sandown Bay to the gleaming white steeps of Culver. We have it on the authority of the *Guide to Watering Places* that this hill at one time underwent some remarkable changes:

> Sixty or seventy years since, Shanklin Down was not to be discerned from St Catherine's, owing to the intervention of Week Down, whose magnitude and elevation completely concealed it. A gradual but imperceptable expansion, however, of Shanklin Down, has now reared it to a greater bulk, and a greater height by at least a hundred feet, than that of its former invidious neighbour.

The coastline at Ventnor—entertainingly and almost alarmingly sited on the slopes of the Undercliff, is described by Lawrence Wilson:

> . . . on a patch only 400 yards wide of rocks, slides, humps, chutes and hollows, Ventnor clings defiantly like a cluster of manmade barnacles.

One guidebook likens the town to a theatre:

> . . . so that the occupants of every seat, no matter how far back or removed, have a full view of the stage, which in this case is the sea.

The houses look down on the roofs of the tier below, the streets and paths between are steep. In fact it has been said that the St Alban's Steps 'can be confidently recommended as a training ground to aspiring mountaineers'.

Setting out westwards from this striking town along a footpath on the seaward edge of the Undercliff, one can see the rocks of the ancient cliffline walling in the chalk downs above and beyond. There are houses on the Undercliff behind the fields and the main road from Ventnor to the west also goes this way. At one time this road continued round St Catherine's Point to Blackgang, but after a landslip had blocked it in 1928 a new road was driven from Niton over a shoulder of the chalk downs above.

At Blackgang is the best-known of the chines, though the valley here does not run down to the sea but terminates half way down the cliff, cut off from the beach by rock falls. The early Victorian guidebooks described it in extravagant terms:

> . . . a vast and horrible opening, probably effected by some convulsion of the earth. . . . On the shore is a rugged precipice forty feet high, over which the water devolves itself. . . . Nearby is a singular echo, where two speakers, properly placed, hear the reverberation of each other's voice, but not of their own. . . . On the beach is a landslide, an interesting and awful spectacle.

Nowadays it is quite different—a showpiece taking the form of near-vertical parkland with gardens and flowers, a model village, smugglers' cave, hall of mirrors, museum and so on—a popular place of pilgrimage pleasant enough out of season. From Observation Point there are views up and down the coast, the lowest paths looking almost vertically down to the boulder-strewn beach. Perhaps the latter can be reached by a coasteering traverse from one or other side, but it would be necessary to keep an eye on the stability of the rocks above, which here are clays and sandstones of the Lower Greensand.

The next 10 miles of coastline to Freshwater have a cliff edge footpath all the way, while the road runs parallel a quarter of a mile or so inland. There are no villages near the coast but the holiday camps and the accessibility of the beaches from the road mean that this stretch is heavily populated in the summer months. Past Whale Chine to Atherfield Point the rocks are Lower Greensand, then the Wealden beds come in as far as Compton Chine. There are no considerable steep cliffs and almost certainly no climbable rocks, while it is unlikely that a traverse of the beach will present any special problems for the coasteer. At Hanover Point the so-called Pine Raft—trunks of coniferous trees lying in a bed of hard sandstone—is visible at low tide. After Compton Chine steep chalk cliffs lead on to Freshwater.

Freshwater is magnificently sited at sea level in a gap between high vertical chalk cliffs. To the east of the bay are two offshore stacks—Arched Rock, named for its shape, and Stag Rock, to which (in less denuded times perhaps) such an animal is said to have leapt to avoid pursuers. Either could be ascended by special tactics such as a rope projected over the summit, subsequently climbed or used to draw up a rope ladder, or perhaps more straightforwardly. In any case the sea birds in residence would be likely to object. On the west side of the bay is Freshwater Cave which can be explored at low water. The author of the *Guide to Watering Places* was impressed by this:

> . . . an excavation made beneath a lofty cliff, by the constant assault of the sea. The entrance is narrow, but the depth is forty yards; and the passage is strewed with fragments of rock, while the roof is hung with terrific masses, threatening to fall at any moment. A lofty rugged arch admits light to its innermost recesses and thus lessens the horrors of the scene.

In these fenced-off times the only way to see the Needles is to make the trip by boat from Freshwater. A variety of caves—Neptune's Cave, Bar Cave, Frenchman's Hole, Lord Holmes's Parlour—and rock pinnacles—Wedge Rock, Old Pepper Rock—are passed *en route*, culminating in the fine scenery of Scratchell's Bay, where the Grand Arch 200 ft high is one of the finest on our coasts. Climbing was done hereabouts by John Stogdon more than a century ago.

At present the Needles comprise three massive and blunt chalk teeth with the lighthouse (80 ft high, built in 1858) perched on a reef alongside the outer one. It was not always so. At one time there was a tall, slender, in fact remarkably needle-like column, said to have been 180 ft high. This fell in 1784 with a crash heard as far away as Southampton. In recent years a climbing party which attacked the highest of the pinnacles had their activities reported in the *Daily Telegraph*. The three climbers took two hours to reach the top, where they left a flag with 'three sheaves of corn on a red ground'; they took a further two hours over the descent and left in a motor boat. The mystery of their identities was solved a few days later when one of them wrote to the newspaper claiming the ascent for the Wye College Exploration Society; however they did not say how hard it was.

There would seem to be some prospect of a sporting coasteering traverse round the shore from Freshwater to Alum Bay. This is about 4 miles and would require careful planning and close attention to the tides; but it would probably not be allowed anyway.

Round the corner beyond a short stretch of chalk cliff is the famous Alum Bay, chief place of pilgrimage on the island. Soft rocks outcrop here in a succession of almost vertical strata. There is a wide range of colours—black, white, green, yellow, red etc— all breaking up easily into powdery sand. Samples are on sale, as are a variety of sand-filled objects. There is nothing for the climber. Hatherwood Point to the north can be traversed on the beach, then the built-up areas of Totland and Colwell Bays follow. The Solent here is less than 1 mile wide, narrowed by the Hurst Castle shingle spit projecting opposite. A footpath leads on to Yarmouth, yachting centre with a King Henry VIII coastal defence castle.

Beyond the town we continue past Bouldner Cliff to Hamstead, another notable fossil site, until finally the way is blocked by the wide, partially silted-up estuary of the Newtown River, which entails a detour inland. A very deserted piece of coast continues round Thorness Bay to the urban area of West and East Cowes on either side of the Medina River, the former a notable yachting centre, the latter industrial fount of ships and hovercraft. There are King Henry VIII castles, and Queen Victoria's Osborne House is close at hand behind East Cowes.

From this point round past Ryde to Bembridge there seems little to interest the coasteer. Plenty of walking is available within sight of the sea, which is specially interesting because of the passing of ships, great and small, warlike and otherwise, but the countryside is mostly formal and built over. At Whitecliff Bay under the north of Bembridge Down the geological formations are reminiscent of Alum Bay. Culver Cliff itself has been used for climbing, among others by the poet Swinburne:

> Also, being bred by the sea, I was a good cragsman, and am vain to this day of having scaled a well-known cliff on the South Coast; ever before and ever since reputed to be inaccessible.

In 1930 two experienced climbers traversed all round the headland at the cliff foot. They found the rock weathered quite hard near the sea and had an excellent climb taking several hours. 'The crux', writes one of them, 'was a hand traverse. I came off and landed in the sea at the first attempt, but managed it afterwards'. While climbing naked with their clothes strapped to their heads, a rescue boat came to take them off, but they managed to complete the route without seaborne aid.

Further on towards Sandown, where the chalk gives way to sandstone, there is a cave—Hermit's Hole. Sandown and Shanklin are contiguous holiday resorts with fine sands. Shanklin marks the start of the Undercliff, and the chines here and at Luccombe are justly famous. The sandstone outcrops in impressive walls, unfortunately not suitable for rock climbing. Between Luccombe and Bonchurch the Undercliff is particularly wild and tumbled and there is a luxuriant cover of vegetation. In the higher part, amidst all the plants and the wild flowers, is the Devil's Chimney, a deep cleft in the top-most rock wall with a stepped path rising up through it. The setting is reminiscent of High Rocks at Tunbridge Wells at the end of a long rainy spell, and it is just possible that a similar chimney climb could be made here at the front of the cleft by a climber in his oldest clothes. Lower down the cliff there are rocks and caves and a Smugglers' Path; the last big landslide here was in 1818. Once around Dunnose, we are back again among the sheltered steeps of Ventnor, the coastal circuit of the island being about 70 miles.

During the summer months the Isle of Wight is certainly not for the climber, but out of season he will find much there that is entertaining. The hill walks are gentle and secluded, the clifftop walk likewise for some of the way, and the signposting of footpaths is highly developed everywhere. There is no rock that is definitely climbable, but there are prospects of traverses in the areas of steep chalk, as well as certain chalk pinnacles and caves. In, say, April it is far less crowded than the mainland—a very quiet, pleasant and varied countryside.

* * *

Subsequent to the folding and doming of the chalk and other strata of south-east England, further sediments were deposited in the synclines, producing the major physical features known today as the London and the Hampshire Basins. As we have seen, there are young rocks of this period in the northern part of the Isle of Wight and these, though cut off from the remainder by the encroachment of the sea into the Solent River, were originally part of the Hampshire Basin. The basin is almost entirely enclosed by chalk downs—the central ridge of the Isle of Wight, the Purbeck Hills, the downs of Dorset, Cranborne Chase and the downs of Wiltshire and Hampshire. North of the Solent, west of Southampton Water, 144 square miles are occupied by the ancient New Forest. Further west the Wessex Heathlands, Egdon Heath of Thomas Hardy, stretch on nearly to Dorchester.

In the New Forest area there are three types of surface form, each with its characteristic vegetation cover. The higher land consists of plains of gravel which are infertile heathlands with only a few trees. The highest point, around 420 ft, is close to the junction of B3078 and B3079 between Cadnam and Downton. On the long gentle slopes between these plateaux older geological formations are exposed, the land is well drained and fertile and here are the principal woodlands of beech, oak, yew, holly etc. Finally there are lower-lying areas of marshland, poorly drained, with elder, willow, heath, bracken, sedge, bog moss and cotton grass, and in places peat. The whole area was set aside for hunting by decree of William the Conqueror in 1087. There would seem to be no truth in the popular story that he dispossessed and drove out the Saxon inhabitants for this purpose; it is probable that this has always been useless agricultural ground. The inner depths have remained relatively unchanged ever since, so that it has been described as 'a miraculous survival of pre-Norman England'. Rufus the Red King, son of William, was killed in the forest, whether by accident or by murder remains unknown. The Rufus Stone which marks the spot lies by Canterton, 2 miles west of Cadnam; his ghost is said to haunt these woodlands still.

The forest only touches the coast in two small stretches—the first on Southampton Water is now much built over, the second running down to the Solent includes the mouth of the Beaulieu River and the famous Buckler's Hard, where wooden warships were once built from the local trees. Nearby at Beaulieu are the ruins of a famous abbey of the thirteenth century. To the west of Milford soft sandy cliffs in these young rocks, which continue as far as the Dorset border, are built over most of the way. Hengistbury Head by Christchurch harbour reaches 119 ft and the height also exceeds 100 ft by Barton; there are chines like those of the Isle of Wight.

In 1924 the Forestry Commission took over control and the whole is now a National Forest Park—preserved (we must hope) for its flora and fauna and the public enjoyment thereof. Three main highways cross from side to side—the A31 trunk road from Cadnam to Ringwood, the A35 from Southampton to Bournemouth and the A337 from Cadnam to Lymington; the main line railway between Southampton and Bournemouth likewise. The only sizeable towns are Lyndhurst and Brockenhurst. Thus, while a significant cross-section of the forest is available to the motorist who can penetrate still further on minor roads between the others, the true appreciation that this is the largest and wildest area of unenclosed land in the South East can only come to the walker on the paths and rides through the woods and across the heaths. This is fine walking country for the climber even though there are no considerable eminences. The land form is of a block rather than a ridge, or ridges, so that there is no watershed walk that can be recommended for its views. The Forestry Commission's guidebook describes a number of routes of 6–8 miles which together cover the range of what the forest has to offer.

On no account should the traveller miss the Arboreta—the Bolderwood near the Lyndhurst–Ringwood road and the Ornamental Drive at Rhinefield Lodge by Brockenhurst. At both sites there are sequoias of close on 150 ft with girths, measured at 4 ft 3 in above the ground, of more than 20 ft. A Douglas Fir at Bolderwood tops 150 ft, while numerous other varieties reach to over 100 ft. In William the Conqueror's time the beasts of the forest included wild boar and wolf; now the largest are the deer of which there are four species—Fallow, Roe, Sika and Red Deer. Smaller animals include fox, badger, otter, stoat, weasel, various mice—and the famous ponies. The traveller interested in reptiles and amphibians will find all native British species in the forest, namely three snakes (Adder, Grass Snake and Smooth Snake), three lizards (Sand and Heath Lizards, and Slow Worm), two toads (Common and Natterjack), the common frog and three newts.

Camping is allowed in the forest under carefully controlled conditions of site and permit; it is excellent country for this purpose.

Egdon Heath stretches westwards—'haggard Egdon . . . the storm was its lover, the wind its friend'. The heath country of Bournemouth and its hinterland continues past Wareham and along the south side of Poole Harbour, its southern limit here sharply demarcated by the Purbeck Hills. On Studland Heath, north of Swanage, is the Agglestone, or Devil's Night Cap, a sandstone boulder 15 ft high, where several climbs have been made. Southwest of Wareham the military are firmly in control. The public is excluded from the great gun ranges below the Purbeck Hills and from several miles of the coast, while the hills themselves can only be traversed on one road. West of Wareham is Bovington Camp with a tank museum, the surrounding heath cut up and turned almost to a desert by tracked vehicles. Nearby on Winfrith Heath is an experimental Atomic Power Station. These western heaths therefore have not much left to offer the visiting climber, who, in spite of various access restrictions, will find more to attract him on the coastline a few miles to the south. This heath country terminates against the chalk hills around Dorchester.

G

6

SALISBURY PLAIN

A GLANCE at the geological map of south-east England will show that the chalk outcrop takes the form of a series of arms or ridges radiating from a central hub which coincides more or less with the county of Wiltshire. North-eastwards the Berkshire Downs and the Chilterns lead on to the East Anglian Heights and the Norfolk coast of the Wash. To the east are the Hampshire Downs and beyond them the North and South Downs spread ever further apart embracing between them, as we have seen, the varied terrain of the Weald. To the south-west a shorter arm follows Cranborne Chase into Dorset and then bifurcates—one branch running east through the Isle of Purbeck to Swanage Bay, the other west reaching as far as Devonshire. In the days when the surrounding valleys were largely impenetrable forest, thicket and marsh, the chalk uplands provided home sites and food for the people, while the ridges interconnected the various communities and gave them access to the sea. Ridgeways along other rock types also formed part of the network; thus access from this central area to the Bristol Channel and Wales followed the Mountain Limestone ridge of the Mendips to the sea at Worlebury by Weston-super-Mare, while the Cotswolds provided a highway towards the Midlands and the North. After looking at Salisbury Plain, the great cross-roads of prehistoric Britain, the next chapter will conduct the traveller ever northwards and eastwards along the line of the greatest of the ridgeways into East Anglia.

The bounds of Salisbury Plain are roughly circular with a diameter of 30–40 miles. It is a countryside of great distances which inspires lyrical prose from its guide-writers:

> . . . an ocean suddenly frozen, as it were, into green cliffs whose pastoral escarpments guard the valleys and vales like giant fortifications. (David Verey)
> Salisbury Plain is like the sea. The blue-rimmed clouds which detach themselves from the blue horizon and sail unhurriedly across

the zenith are like those which rise up from the sea. The undulating
turf, grey-blue with distance, resembles petrified billows of some
immense ocean. The beech-crowned hill-tops are atolls bravely defy-
ing the heaving waves. (Ralph Whitlock)

Unfortunately the beauty is largely sham as far as the modern
foot traveller is concerned, for approximately one third of the whole
area is in the hands of government departments and given over
to permanent military camps, ranges and manœuvring grounds,
aerodromes and other defence establishments. The walker will be
hastened on his way by rifle fire, tanks, artillery, jet aircraft and
other fearsome accompaniments of our civilisation, so that it is
hardly walking country; yet to drive across can be pleasant enough.
Military occupation began in 1897, the War Department owned
over 40,000 acres by 1902 and, after two total wars, over 80,000
acres by 1953. The military keep exclusive use of half of this;
occasional use of the rest is permitted to other interests. Noteworthy
in one of the larger cut-off areas is the village of Imber, once a
delightful spot far from railway stations and main roads, now a
ruin used for practice in street fighting.

The Plain is drained by five rivers, likened of course to the
fingers of a hand because they meet in the south-east in the neighbourhood of Salisbury—the Ebble, the Nadder, the Wylye, the Avon
and the Bourne. The predominating surface rock is chalk though
only occasionally do we find the steep scarp slopes which characterise this rock elsewhere. However a wedge of limestone and
greensand running along the Nadder Valley from a base between
Shaftesbury and Mere reaches almost to Barford St Martin.

The hills south of the Ebble run from near Salisbury down to
Cranborne Chase. The ridgetop route here, called the Ox Drove,
leads over Marleycombe Hill, past Winklebury Camp, to Win
Green Hill near the Dorset border, the highest point of the Chase.
Further north the ridge between the Ebble and the Nadder carries
another trackway, the Salisbury Way, which can be followed from
near Salisbury, past Castle Ditches and Chiselbury Camp, to White
Sheet Hill above Berwick St John. On the northern scarp face
above the A30 trunk road, modern figures carved on the chalk
hillsides include a number of regimental badges, a map of Australia,
a rising sun, and so on. Broadly speaking these hill lines terminate
abruptly in the west at a scarp line which looks out over the valley
of the Stour.

The limestone which outcrops in the Nadder Valley between the chalk hills has been quarried at Chilmark for a building stone used in Salisbury and Chichester Cathedrals. A hole in the hillside leads into 13 acres of large vaults and passages, in places 80 ft high, with roof supported by pillars. Unfortunately the military now occupy this interesting site and access is not allowed. The village of Teffont Evias nearby has a notable link with climbing and particularly with coasteering; here nearly 100 years ago Arthur Westlake Andrews, later a leading British rock climber and the father of the new sport of coasteering, spent his childhood climbing on the local trees and walking in the local hills.

The trackway which traversed the ridge between the valleys of the Nadder and the Wylye, known as the Grovely Ridge Way, was part of the ancient route from the Kent coast to the Mendips and the Bristol Channel. The hills reach their greatest height in the extreme west near Maiden Bradley, almost in Somerset, where Long Knoll is 944 ft. There is a fine hill walk of some 20 miles around Maiden Bradley, coinciding in part with the circuit formerly traced out by the villagers in 'beating the bounds' of the parish. The boundary itself takes in Brimsdown Hill, Rodmead Hill and Long Knoll (which has a view from the Bristol Channel to the English Channel including the Cotswolds, the Purbeck Hills and Exmoor); other hills could be added to the circuit as required.

The wedge of the plain between the Wylye and the Avon is largely under military occupation with just one north-south road (A360 from Devizes to Shrewton). It is highest in the north-west and slopes gently across towards Salisbury. The steep scarp facing west and north towards the Somerset Avon carries the carved figure of the Westbury White Horse (restored in 1778, replacing an earlier model) and camps at Scratchbury and Battlesbury above Warminster and Bratton Castle above Bratton. Further east the same scarp becomes the south wall of the Vale of Pewsey. 'Inland' are the forlorn ruins at Imber and relics of even earlier man now unfortunately inaccessible. Still within our reach however is the majestic ruin of Stonehenge, a very popular place of pilgrimage.

There are on Salisbury Plain, says Michael Drayton:

> . . . stones of huge weight and greatness, some in the earth pitched, and in form erected, as it were circular; others lying cross over them, as if their own poise did no less than their supporters give them that proper place, have this name of Stone-henge.

In those times men did not understand the purpose or the meaning of the henge; even now after centuries of archaeological investigation we are still not quite sure—temple, cathedral, astronomical clock of the seasons, or what?

The first written mention is thought to have been in 400 BC by Hecateus, a Greek:

> The Hyperboreans have in their Island a sacred enclosure dedicated to Apollo, as well as a magnificent circular temple adorned with rich offerings.

Geoffrey of Monmouth in the twelfth century told how Merlin brought some of the stones from Ireland by magic, a story with a factual basis for certain of them were in fact brought from Prescelley Mountain in Pembrokeshire, by route and method unknown. The remainder are Sarsen Stones, sandstone boulders which litter the surface of the chalk downs both here and further north. The circle is dwarfed by the immensity of the plain and appears insignificant from afar. Close at hand it impresses: one marvels at the ingenuity of the builders, who in the years between 1900 and 1400 BC wrought all this with primitive tools such as flints and deer antlers. The complex history of the actual stages of the building has been unravelled by archaeologists. The henge comprised concentric circles and horseshoes of the two building stones, trilithons (uprights with a stone laid on top like a doorway), a circular earthwork and an avenue. Many stones have fallen but an impressive array remains.

Now there are car parks, kiosks and all the appurtenances of the motorist civilisation; a barbed wire fence prevents illegal entry and removal of the stones and discourages desecration and defacement. The upkeep is in the capable hands of the Ministry of Works. Come with all the others on a warm summer's afternoon and you are looking through a modern window at a curious detached relic of the remote past which hardly impinges at all. Come to it across the plain at sundown on a stormy winter's day, rain clouds speeding across the vast sky above—the modern world drops away and you are contemporary with these great stones, fearful of their purpose and the stories they have to tell.

The wedge of country between the Avon and the Bourne is heavily militarised with great modern camps at Tidworth and Bulford; the Bulford Kiwi cut by New Zealand soldiers of the first world war is one of the largest of modern chalk figures—420 ft long and covering 1½ acres. Once again the land is highest in the north above Pewsey and slopes gently towards the south. The trackways here led to the ancient site of Old Sarum on the hills above Salisbury. At one time this was a city built within the bounds of an Iron Age camp; the extensive earthworks covering 27 acres remain, as does the mound of the Norman castle, but only fragments of the castle itself and the cathedral. Salisbury was built in the valley below during the thirteenth century; the cathedral at Old Sarum was abandoned in 1327, though it was still visible four centuries later when Stukeley passed this way. The castle did not survive the Wars of the Roses and, in fact, in the course of time all the ruins became a source of stone for local building. There is a fine view from here of the city and the Plain.

The slender spire of Salisbury Cathedral, erected over a century later than the main bulk of the building, reaches 404 ft. In Europe only Strasbourg and Amiens are higher. Its construction set up great strains in the fabric and the top is now about 2 ft out of perpendicular. Many years ago climbing used to be done on the roof and the spire, as Ralph Whitlock tells us:

> Apparently at one time Salisbury's old Whitsuntide Fair (now fallen into disuse and forgotten) was held in the Close, and its closing days seem to have been marked by hair-raising expeditions over the roofs of the Cathedral and up the spire. Stegophily is evidently not essentially a modern craze, and the thought of half-drunken young gallants clambering about those giddy pinnacles makes us marvel that we do not have a long record of fatal accidents.

An anonymous contributor to *Oxford and Cambridge Mountaineering* in 1924 described the cathedral as 'the finest rock outcrop on the chalk downs'. In the very finest traditions of armchair mountaineering he went on to detail the lines of possible ascents on the west front and the walls of the nave, passing finally to the spire:

> The best climbs are to be found on and around the spire, which is full-blown Decorated Gothic. At each corner of the top of the tower, where the spire leaves it, are to be found two ornate pinnacles —upper and lower. The lower are perfectly easy though loose. The upper are more interesting. It is necessary first to stand on the parapet of the tower and then step across into the rather vague chimney between the spire and pinnacle. Back-and-foot work at a

rather insecure angle then follows. A fall, however would (probably) be checked by the parapet.

The main peak forms a single pitch some 150 feet in height, and, being octagonal, may be attempted via any of its eight buttresses. All are very loose. Large holds at six inch intervals are provided by the ball-flower ornamentation of the arêtes; the climbs differ only in the varying numbers of balls which are missing. Though very steep and exposed, they are of no technical difficulty, and were frequently climbed during the Middle Ages by persons in a condition of partial inebriation. . . . Of late centuries, however, the climb has become more severe owing to the deterioration of the rock. Also there are no belays, and any failure of balance, or of the ball-flowers, would involve a fall outwards over the parapet of from 250 to 400 feet, broken only by purely temporary contact with the cathedral roof. The ideal party for this climb would seem to number eight; one climber could then attack each arête and all be secured by one rope, passing completely round the spire and shortened as the climb proceeded.

North of Salisbury Plain, between it and the Marlborough Downs, lies the Vale of Pewsey which takes the form of a hanging valley in the chalk facing towards the west, even though there is no west flowing stream along its length. The vale shows in fact a miniature of the structure of the Weald and results from the erosion of a one-time dome or fold in the chalk, which has left scarp slopes on either side of the valley, while exposing Upper Greensand on the floor. The drainage, which was initiated before the country arrived at its present form, appears, as we have seen in the Weald, to be arbitrary at first sight. Streams flowing from the east and west join and, breaching the south wall of the valley, flow southwards as the River Avon to Salisbury and Christchurch Bay. The length of the vale is traversed, not only by the Western Region main line but also by the former Kennet-Avon Canal, now alas impassable except for canoes. The canal climbs from Hungerford by nineteen locks to a tunnel south of Savernake, then four more locks lead to the summit level—a long pound of 15 miles. On the far side the canal descends below Devizes by a notable staircase of locks, no less than twenty-nine in 1¼ miles. The chalk scarp slopes, particularly those to the north at the western end below Tan Hill, Milk Hill, and so on, are among the most impressive in the country. Milk Hill at 964 ft is the county summit of Wiltshire. Tan Hill, previously adjudged lower, is also credited with 964 ft on the latest OS map, while Martinsell Hill at the eastern end of the scarp is also above 900 ft. Etchilhampton Hill (623 ft), an isolated peak above Devizes, is also noteworthy. All this is fine walking country. The south wall of the vale nowhere reaches 800 ft so that the high summits in the north have expansive views over towards Salisbury Plain, the mound of Old Sarum and Salisbury Cathedral spire. There are two white horses—one above Alton Barnes close to Milk Hill, cut in 1812, the other above Pewsey village on Pewsey Hill, cut in 1937 to replace an earlier partially obliterated figure dating back to 1785.

At the 'head' of the Vale of Pewsey, south and east of Marlborough, lies the ancient forest of Savernake, traversed along its northern fringes by the A4 trunk road from Newbury. This was medieval hunting country, held by the king and administered under his Forest Laws. William I appointed the first wardens in 1083 and the forest has remained under the care of descendants of the same family up to the present time. The woodlands we see today are the result of continued planned cultivation having slowly replaced the straggling woods, the grass and heather roughlands and the downland which formerly covered the site. The present circumference is around 16 miles. The Grand Avenue has a length of 4 miles with eight paths or roads meeting at its centre. Climbers will be interested to be reminded that a route made on Raven Crag, Langdale, in 1943 was named Savernake, a name presumably descriptive of its scenery.

Before setting out on the long journey by the ancient trackways to East Anglia, we turn aside for a moment to look at the ridge lines connecting Salisbury Plain with the North and South Downs. South of the Kennet, which flows through Hungerford and Newbury to join the Thames at Reading, is an outstanding range of hills where the chalk reaches its greatest altitude in England. The first high hill is Wexcombe Down (874 ft), a mile or two east of the headwaters of the Bourne; the ridge leads on over a hill of 860 ft to Fosbury Camp on Heydown Hill. A low pass follows between the head of the Bourne Rivulet (a tributary of the Test) and the watershed of the Kennet and the Avon. In early days this would have provided a dry route northwards avoiding the marshy valley of the Kennet. From Botley Hill a well-defined scarp runs east for some 16 miles to Cottington's Hill above Kingsclere. Along Rivar Down and over Ham Hill we reach Inkpen Hill, which, long credited with 1,011 ft, was demoted just before the turn of the century to 955 ft. When this state of affairs was finally accepted, the Berkshire authorities are said to have shifted the border with Hampshire so as to bring Walbury Hill within their boundaries and thus retain the summit hill of the range. Half a mile on is Combe Gibbet, which is maintained under the terms of the lease of a nearby farm; it certainly presents an eerie spectacle when decorated with a scarecrow hanging from its topmost limb. Some of the southern valleys cut back deeply into the hills hereabouts and in the neighbourhood of the Gibbet the ridge is almost equally steep on either side. The minor road from Inkpen to Combe gives easy access to these hills.

East of this road is Walbury Hill (974 ft), county summit of Berkshire, the highest chalk hill in England and the highest point within the 80-mile circle round London. The bank and ditch of the summit camp have a circumference of 1 mile. The top of the hill, flat and cultivated, is not particularly distinguished—certainly the most shapely and most memorable chalk hills are not on these undulating scarped ridges but isolated peaks like Pitstone Hill or Mount Caburn. However, this one is higher than them all. Combe Hill, the next high point on the ridge, lies back somewhat from the edge. Soon the Berkshire-Hampshire border, which has climbed from West Woodhay in the valley and traversed the scarp edge for a mile, swings away to the south and the next hill, 2 miles from Walbury, is Pilot Hill (937 ft), the county summit of Hampshire. There is a possible basis for a long-distance walk here in which the county summits of Hampshire (Pilot Hill), Berkshire (Walbury Hill) and Wiltshire (Milk Hill/Tan Hill) could be traversed in a single expedition of some 20 miles along this scarp and the northern rim of the Vale of Pewsey.

Our route continues eastwards and, after crossing A343 at close on 800 ft, we find the scarp running southwards to Seven Barrows on A34 where there is a low pass across the range. The prominent Beacon Hill (858 ft) is an outlier strongly fortified by ramparts on the 800 ft contour. Rather more than a mile away on the far side of the road, the camp on Ladle Hill is of special interest because it was never finished, so that archaeologists have been able to learn something of the methods of constructing these hill forts from an examination of its banks and ditches. Cottington's Hill beyond B3051 is the last point above 700 ft and marks the end of this long and distinctive route. Though this is a specially attractive walk for us today it was only a minor way for the early traveller. The main highway of the Harrowway lies further south, often coinciding with present-day minor roads; from Stonehenge it passed north of Amesbury, south of Weyhill, north of Andover and Whitchurch and south of Basingstoke, thence to Farnham, the Hog's Back and by the North Downs to the Channel coast.

The route which connected the Salisbury Plain area with the South Downs, setting off south-east from Salisbury over Dean Hill, soon passes into Hampshire. There is no definite ridgeway for the next few miles, though beyond the Test the way crossed Farley Mount to Winchester. Unlike that of Salisbury, the cathedral here would appear to have no open associations with climbing. Leaving by Deacon Hill and Telegraph Hill we continue to another Beacon Hill, and crossing the Meon Valley, reach Old Winchester Hill (672 ft), a notable archaeological site now in the charge of the Nature Conservancy. Butser Hill, the starting point of the South Downs, is only a few miles ahead and the ridgeway thenceforward is open all the way to Beachy Head.

Setting out on the journey along the Great Ridgeway from Alton Priors in the Vale of Pewsey, we go through the pass between Milk Hill and Knap Hill. The way has already traversed many miles of hill country from Axmouth in far-off Devonshire past Pilsdon Pen, Lewesdon Hill, the Cerne Abbas Giant, Bulbarrow Hill, Hod and Hambledon Hills and Win Green Hill and through the war-torn plain around Imber. All the routes I have mentioned, and indeed many others hereabouts, are delineated in *Ancient Trackways of Wessex* by H. W. Timperley and Edith Brill which is a guide and companion for anyone hill walking in this ancient kingdom. Soon the Wansdyke is reached, dug in the fifth century to hold back the Saxons pressing forward from the north and east. Possibly the best-preserved section of the dyke is found here between Morgan's Hill, south-east of Calne, and Savernake Forest. To the north are the headwaters of the Kennet, rich with achaeological remains including the outstanding stone circle at Avebury, Silbury Hill, West Kennet Long Barrow and Windmill Hill Camp. There are white horses on Granham Hill, south-west of Marlborough, and on Cherhill Down over towards Calne. All these downs are used extensively for the training of race-horses.

The Circle at Avebury was constructed between 1700 and 1500 BC. A circular earth bank threequarters of a mile in circumference encloses 29 acres of level ground. Inside is a great ditch originally 50 ft below the top of the bank; encircling its inner edge is a line of large stones. Stukeley in 1722 found forty-four stones standing and could trace the sites of around a hundred more. Now only eighteen remain. The modern village stands within the ditch and much of its building material was derived from the circle. The stones are local sarsens, neither chiselled nor shaped, and in no circumstances should they be climbed upon. From the south side an avenue of pairs of stones leads to the site of another stone circle, the Sanctuary, on Overton Hill just over a mile away. The whole is tremendously impressive and should on no account be missed. A mile to the south over against the Bath road is Silbury Hill, said to be the largest artificial hill in Europe. It is 130 ft high and has a diameter of 110 ft at the top, the base covering 5 acres. However one would imagine that many a slag heap, china-clay spoil heap or slate tip would exceed these dimensions comfortably. No one knows its purpose—a burial mound, a shadow hill to mark the progress of the sun and thus determine dates for seed time and harvest? It remains a mystery monument. Beyond the Bath road the West Kennet Long Barrow, the largest in England, is under the charge of the Ministry of Works, as are the Avebury site and the nearby museum. One and a quarter miles north-west, Windmill Hill, with its camp dating back to about 2500 BC, has given its name to a period of Neolithic culture. This is a fine example of the so-called causewayed camp, used to shelter cattle and as a dwelling, not as a fort.

The chalk country north of the Bath road exhibits two scarp edges separated by a plateau of 550–650 ft. The more westerly scarp drops from this level towards the tributaries of the Somerset Avon. There is a white horse here on Broadtown Down close to B4041. The easterly scarp forms the edge of Marlborough Downs, which reach 892 ft at Hackpen Hill. There is another white horse here and yet another on Rockley Down 2 miles nearer Marlborough.

During our travels through the downlands of Wiltshire we have passed a number of these cut figures of horses—eight to be exact. These could be linked together in a White Horse Walk which would take the traveller some 45–50 miles through the best scenery in the county. Starting with the Westbury horse above Bratton, we traverse the north edge of the plain for some 20 miles to the Pewsey;

now north-west for 6 miles across the Vale of Pewsey to the Alton Barnes, then back north-east for another 6 miles to the Granham Hill. Luckily the Marlborough Downs horses are close together and the next 8 miles see us past the Rockley and the Hackpen Hill to the Broadtown Down; a final leg of 6 miles to the south-west leads to a finish at the Cherhill Down. None of these has the great antiquity of the Uffington White Horse which we shall pass in due course on the Great Ridgeway. Westbury and Cherhill are eighteenth-century, Rockley uncertain—late eighteenth- or early nineteenth-century—the remainder nineteenth except for Pewsey, which is a youngster dating only from 1937.

7

THE GREAT RIDGEWAY

WE set out now on the Great Ridgeway, the ancient route along
the chalk hills to East Anglia. The way has already traversed many
miles of hill country from Axmouth in far-off Devonshire past
Pilsdon Pen, Lewesdon Hill, the Cerne Abbas Giant, Bulbarrow
Hill, Hod and Hambledon Hills and Win Green Hill, and through
the war-torn plain around Imber. It has crossed the Vale of Pewsey
by Alton Priors, threaded the pass between Milk Hill and Knap
Hill, crossed the Wansdyke and so brought us here to the ancient
area of Avebury.

We cross the Bath road near the site of the Sanctuary on Overton
Hill and climb away northward up Avebury Down. The hillsides
to the east are plentifully scattered with sarsen stones, otherwise
grey wethers (because of a distant resemblance to sheep), Druid
stones or bridestones—blocks of sandstone, the harder remnants
of a bed which formerly covered the whole area. No doubt it was
the existence of these massive boulders that encouraged the early
builders of circles and barrows to site them hereabouts, while the
shapes of the stones determined to some extent the nature of the
finished constructions. The map shows a tremendous accumulation
of them on Overton Down and Fyfield Down, while to the south
the National Trust preserves two small typical areas at Lockeridge
Dene and Piggle Dene. The Ridgeway climbs on over Hackpen
Hill, then, swinging north-east, it runs down past Barbury Castle
to cross A345 at Chiseldown. Ahead at over 900 ft are the banks
of Liddington Castle; our route skirts the hillside below and crossing A419 runs on to Fox Hill, where a pass crosses the range.

A spendid section of hilltop trackway runs from here to Streatley
beside the Thames more than 20 miles away. The steep combes
hollowed out of the scarp face are a special feature. We soon reach
the first of these above Bishopstone, at the head of which is an
impressive series of lynchets—banks marking the site of Neolithic

125

cultivation. Hippisley Cox describes these as 'the best specimens of "Shepherds' Steeps" in the whole course of the Ridgeway, or indeed the whole down country'. Crossing from Wiltshire into Berkshire we reach Wayland Smith's Cave, a denuded long barrow with the stone chamber exposed.

We press on along Drayton's 'lusty rising Downs', a widespread view towards Midland England on our left hand. On clear days, says Hippisley Cox, 'the smoke of Birmingham can be seen more than a hundred miles away'. Immediately below is the Vale of the White Horse with the River Ock; on the far side beyond the Corallian ridge lie the River Thames and the minor heights of Oxfordshire. Uffington Castle is on the top of the Downs at 856 ft. Below it is the most famous and oldest of the white horses—a stylised figure dating back to pre-Roman times of the first or second century BC. G. K. Chesterton made it known to every schoolboy:

> Before the gods that made the gods
> Had seen their sunrise pass,
> The White Horse of the White Horse Vale
> Was cut out of the grass.

It is 365 ft long and 130 ft high. All is accessible by road. Below again is a deep combe, called the Manger, and the small conical Dragon Hill, where St George slew the eponymous beast.

Periodically through its history the local people have cleaned up the outlines of the horse, cutting away the weeds and the runs of mud, and restoring it to some approximation of the original shape. On these occasions a local holiday used to be taken and a fair and games were held in and around Uffington Castle. We are fortunate that Tom Hughes, the author of *Tom Brown's Schooldays*, has left us an account of these jollifications in the year 1857, which in fact turned out to be the last of the series. Thereafter fairs and games retreated to lower levels with other excuses, while cleaning the horse became an uncelebrated routine. *The Scouring of the White Horse* is partly a country and travel book, partly a history— a nostalgic reminder of the days before England's population became too big for her countryside. Hughes's hero sits above the ears of the horse watching the scourers at work:

> The turf was as soft as a feather bed, and as springy as horse-hair; and it was all covered with thistle-down, which came drifting along like snow with the south wind; and all down below the country looked so rich and peaceful, stretching out for miles and

miles at my feet in the hazy sunshine, and the larks right up over-head sang so sweetly, that I didn't know whether to laugh or cry. I should have liked to have had a turn at the besoms and shovels with the men, who seemed very good tempered, only I was too shy, and I couldn't make out half they said. . . .

Next day there were several thousand people on the hill enjoying themselves with picnics and fortune tellers, watching the wrestling and the backsword play, carthorse, donkey and foot races, the chasing and catching of a piglet, and so on. The greased pole with a leg of mutton waiting at the top for the successful climber was attacked by methods which would be accepted as legitimate in modern rock climbing:

> . . . when I got up to it, I saw a heavy-looking fellow standing some five feet up the pole, with one foot in a noose of cord depending from a large gimlet, and the other leg hooked round the pole. He held in his right hand another large gimlet, which he was preparing to screw into the pole to support a second noose, and gazed stolidly down at a Committee-man, who was objecting 'that this wasn't fair climbing—that if gimlets and nooses were to be allowed, he could get up himself'. I thought he was right; but public feeling seemed to side with the climber.

What else, after all, is an *étrier*?

Interesting too was the race down the precipitous slopes of the Manger after a cartwheel which bounded ahead of the runners in great leaps:

> Away go the fourteen men in hot pursuit, gipsies, shepherds and light-heeled fellows of all sorts, helter-skelter; some losing their foot-hold at once, and rolling or slipping down; some still keeping their footing, but tottering at every step; one or two, with their bodies well thrown back, striking their heels firmly into the turf, and keeping a good balance. They are all in the road together, but here several fall on their faces, and others give in; the rest cross it in a moment, and are away down the manger. Here the sheep-walks, which run temptingly along the sides of the manger, but if they would look forward will take the runners very little nearer the bottom where the wheel lies, mislead many; and amongst the rest, the fleetest of the gipsies, who makes off at full speed along one of them. Two or three men go still boldly down the steep descent, falling and picking themselves up again; and Jonathan Legg, of Childrey, is the first of these. He has now gained the flat ground at the bottom, where after a short stagger he brings himself up and makes straight for the umpires, touching the wheel a clear ten yards ahead of his nearest rival.

All this is more than a century past. The road round the upper rim of the Manger, which once knew the thunderous bounce of the flying cartwheel, now carries motor cars to a large viewpoint parking place, whence the modern traveller reaches the hilltop or the ancient chalk horse with hardly a climb at all.

A mile east of Uffington Castle an unusual object below the scarp slope is known as King Alfred's Bugle or the Blowing Stone. As Hughes tells it:

> In front of the inn door was an oak tree, and under the tree a big stone with some curious holes in it, into which pieces of wood were fitted, secured by a padlock and chain. I was wondering what it could be, when the landlord came out with some of his guests, and pulling out a key unlocked the padlock, and took the pieces of wood out of the holes. Then there was some talk between the young men and their sweethearts, and first one and then another stooped down and blew into the hole at the top, and the stone made a dull moaning sound, unlike anything I had ever heard. The landlord told me that when it was well blown on a still day, it could be heard for four or five miles, and I should think it could; for I left them blowing away when I started again, and heard the sound every now and then until I was close up to the Castle, though the wind blew from the south, and down the hill.

Some considerable time later Hippisley Cox described the sound as like a foghorn; 'it is seldom', he says, 'that one of the beautiful girls from the cottage is unwilling to instruct the stranger'.

The road beside the stone marks the line of the ancient Icknield Way, an alternative to the Ridgeway at a lower and less acceptable level. Marching on a parallel track to the Thames at the Goring Gap and beyond, it occupies on these slopes a position somewhat similar to that of the Pilgrims' Way on the North Downs. The Ridgeway continues high above the plains past another great combe, the Devil's Punchbowl, by Letcombe Bassett and past Segsbury Camp to the Wantage–Hungerford road (A338). Between here and the Abingdon–Newbury road (A34), 6 miles to the east, is the Saxon mound of Scutchamer Knob (or Cwichelmes Low). Out in the vale the atomic research station at Harwell is built athwart the Icknield Way—a grim reminder of the precariousness of our very existence. With all our advantages who would not sometimes wish himself back in the England of Hippisley Cox or of Hughes, in the days before our inventions threaten to drive us from our own earth! Now all we can do is to turn the other way; we cross Blewbury Down and soon find the hills falling away at last to Streatley and the Goring Gap, where the River Thames has cut through the chalk ridge on which we have travelled for so many miles.

Between the Vale of the White Horse and the Thames lies a ridge of low hills known as the Faringdon Ridge, or sometimes the Corallian Ridge on account of the fossils in its limestone. This is high pastoral country and only two points exceed 500 ft—Badbury Hill, with a camp, by Faringdon, and Boars Hill looking down on Oxford. The city is cradled in hills, for Wytham Hill to the north-west is 539 ft and Shotover Hill to the east 562 ft. Beside the Thames a few miles Londonwards are the Sinodun Hills, which rise to close on 400 ft by Wallingford. As Leland noted in his travels:

> This place is wonderful dikid about and standith on a hille in Barkshir, hanging over the Tamise. It is yn by estimation half a mile. And withyn it hath beene sum towne, or, as the commune voice sayith, a castelle in the Britannes tyme, defacid by lykelihod by the Danes. At this tyme it berith very plentifullye booth barley and whete, and numismata Romanorum be ther found yn ploughyng.

The upstream hill, Wittenham Clumps, is the higher and has the camp on a spur, the downstream hill is called Brightwell Barrow.

The village of Horspath near Shotover Hill at Oxford occupies a tiny niche in British climbing literature going back to *Oxford and Cambridge Mountaineering*, 1922. Members of the University Mountaineering Club having no local rocks and in those days no ready transport to reach the places described in this book, turned to the local railway bridges for practice sport:

> The discovery of bridge-climbing at Horspath, last autumn, has revealed a pastime which affords a little consolation when Chamonix or even P.y.g. seems far away. A series of bridges cut by roads under an embanked railway line are the places of exercise; the surface of the cutting formed consists of two opposite walls of rough-hewn stone on each side of the bridge proper. As the walls are inclined at seventy five and eighty degrees and the stones are irregular in shape and size, a genuine rock face is practically obtained. The holds are vague and occasional so that each bridge affords a series of severe face pitches about twenty to thirty feet high.

Exploration was carried on energetically throughout the winter and

H

the twenty or so courses mapped out have put no small strain on the resources of the nomenclature. The names are of all kinds ranging from the sweetly domestic associations of the Bratlings Route to the macabre 'Suicides Chimney'. Let us not under-estimate this discovery made on Horspath uplands; no longer shall we forlornly contemplate the passage of a train for some mountain region—we shall approach the line more closely and haply find consolation at the very source of our despair.

What happened here in subsequent years is shrouded in secrecy; climbers gradually acquired the means to travel further afield and the things they found were, as is so often the case, automatically regarded as more worthy of record. Then in 1957 came an account in *Oxford Mountaineering* of routes on a 30 ft brick wall at the entrance to Horspath Tunnel with pictures showing how hard it must be—'it does not cultivate muscle so much as destroy it'. A guidebook description appeared in the same journal in 1960 of what was by now called Horspath Horror, with a diagram showing the exact lines of the thirteen routes. At that time the trains were still providing an additional hazard but in due course Dr Beeching took care of that one. Finally a writer in 1964 directed attention to the bridges on the disused line to Woodstock—'what the climbs lack in height they make up for in objective danger'.

Stegophily, climbing upon buildings, is by a quirk of literary fortune associated much more with Cambridge than with Oxford. Cambridge roofs were described in print by no less than Geoffrey Winthrop Young at the turn of the century and later by the anonymous Whipplesnaith between the wars, but comparable deeds on the more westerly site have remained completely unsung. There was however an article in *Oxford and Cambridge Mountaineering*, 1922, asserting the same order of antiquity for Oxford and there seems little doubt that the efforts and achievements have run closely parallel. This account listed numerous routes which had already been carried out; many more must be known today but each and every climber keeps this sort of information to himself. Says this anonymous author of 1922:

> Roof climbing, like any other sport, should be pursued, if at all, solely for the sake of pleasure derived from it; and if any such pleasure can be said to be derived from the practice, its claim to existence is *ipso facto* established. . . . Apart from the ever-threatening danger presented by officialdom, roof climbing may be regarded as generally more dangerous than any but rock climbs

of exceptional difficulty. To begin with, the roof climber disregards the most rudimentary laws of mountaineering. He seldom takes a rope, and when he does it is almost certain to prove quite useless. Again, the element of uncertainty and instability contributes to the thrill of the whole thing; rotten rock on mountains can usually be tested beforehand, but one can never be certain from the bottom whether a pipe or lightning conductor is firmly fixed at the top, and it is no unusual sensation to feel one hundred-weight or so of masonry rocking beneath one's weight. . . . The perpendicularity of walls, as compared with even the steepest mountain precipices, adds to the difficulty. Forty feet of perpendicular fall pipe presents as exhausting a climb as the most ardent enthusiast can crave.

Roof climbing is not just a special development of rock climbing but is diverse.

In the north-west of Oxfordshire a ridge of limestone, known as marlstone, continues the general line of the Cotswolds. Near Chipping Norton are the Rollright Stones—a prehistoric circle finer than any in England excepting only Stonehenge and Avebury. Stukeley, passing this way in the eighteenth century, wrote of them:

Tis a very Noble Rustic Sight, and Strikes an Odd Terrour into the Spectators, and Admiration of the designers of 'em. It is no small part of the Curiosity to see how these that are left are Coroded like Worm Eaten wood by the harsh Jaws of time. . . .

'Now', says a recent guidebook, 'there are three concentric circles, one of stones, one of fir trees and one of iron railings'. North of Great Rollright village the hills reach 785 ft. Beyond the infant Stour, Brailes Hill (761 ft), which stands in front of the scarp, is in Warwickshire. On ahead the county border runs along the ridge above the Vale of the Red Horse, which gets its name from the only hill figure to have been cut in a rock other than chalk, unfortunately long since obliterated. The scarp slope is steep as we pass along Edge Hill above the field of a famous but inconclusive battle fought in the Civil War in 1642.

The hill line runs ever north-eastwards into Northamptonshire, the county summit of which is Arbury Hill (734 ft), south-west of Daventry. Hereabouts the hills are pierced by canal tunnels at Braunston and Crick; indeed these cultivated hills beset on all sides by industry and routes of communication are often most conveniently explored by canal towpaths, still comparatively lonely and unused. We come to Naseby, which saw the decisive battle of the Civil War in 1645, and these low hills, rolling on towards the north, pass finally outside the area of this chapter.

By now we have diverged considerably from the near straight line of the chalk ridgeway and must hasten back to rejoin it at the Goring Gap. Here we see once again the often repeated phenomenon of the river which seems to turn suddenly, after miles of contented parallel flow, and cut its way through a high chalk ridge. Once again we are looking at a drainage pattern initiated long before the land came to its present form, when the Thames ran off a high dome which has long since been eroded away. The gap is narrow for we cross the bridge between Streatley and Goring and almost immediately begin the climb on to the end of the Chiltern Hills. As John Leland reported to his king:

> Al this way (Henle in Oxfordshire to Wikam in Bukinghamshire to Dunstaple in Bedfordshire) goeth Chilternhilles, whereof many be welle replenishid with wood, and partely with corne, al the soile being a chalke clay.

The scarp edge is not well defined at first and on this side of the Henley–Oxford road (A423) the hills do not quite reach 700 ft. The Icknield Way takes us round past Grim's Ditch and the north-west facing slopes of Ewelme Downs and Swyncombe Downs. The straight line of the scarp begins above Watlington, where the White Mark on the down above belongs to the National Trust. It is a simple figure cut in the chalk in 1764 taking the form of a pyramid nearly 90 ft high and 16 ft across the base. This is Oxfordshire and in the next section of the ridge between here and the A40 trunk road we cross the county summit—Shirburn Hill (835 ft). Though it seems certain that the Great Ridgeway, which we have followed so far over the downs of Wiltshire and Berkshire, continued along the summits of the Chiltern Ridge, little trace of it remains today. The tops are thickly wooded in places though there are some minor roads and tracks. The Icknield Way in the meantime continues its scarp-hugging contouring and has the best of the views unimpeded by the trees. The ridge rolls on by Bold Hill and Beacon Hill where A40 crosses, sloping steeply up the scarp, and on beyond for another 4 miles over Crowell Hill and Chinnor Hill to Bledlow Cross. This is another cut figure which may be ancient or is perhaps only of the eighteenth century.

Now at Wain Hill the scarp turns through a right-angle into a gap through the ridge—an Ice Age spillway for glacier water trapped between these hills and an ice barrier to the north. South-west of the gap is the Bledlow Ridge which runs back for 5 miles to terminate at Church Hill above West Wycombe. H. J. Massing-ham is scathing about the view, and this nearly thirty years ago:

> What the observer sees now from this Darien is the scoop of the valley used as a gigantic rubbish dump. It is a vast dust bin of houses.

The church has a prominent ball on the tower; there is a mausoleum nearby and show caves beneath the hill.

Meanwhile the Icknield Way has crossed the gap and rejoined the scarp below Whiteleaf Cross at Princes Risborough. This one is 50 ft high by 25 ft long with a pyramidal base 340 ft wide. Massingham has no doubts as to its antiquity:

> . . . it has stood or rather leaned against the bluff above the Way from the time when tin ingots on men's shoulders, flints from the factories at Grime's Graves, wool tods on pack-horses, sheep, cattle and ponies, chapmen and pedlars, pilgrims and soldiery passed along the Ridge Way on the summit, first as a solar or phallic sign and from the eighteenth century onwards as a cross.

But once again the modern view tends to ascribe it to the eighteenth century.

We pass on by Pulpit Hill and another Beacon Hill to Coombe Hill (at 852 ft often named as highest point of the range, but in fact not so) and on down to another spillway hill gap at Wendover. Since Bledlow we have been in Buckinghamshire and the highest point of the Chilterns, as well as Buckinghamshire county summit, is now just ahead—Haddington Hill. There is a spot height of 857 ft on the road between Cholesbury and Aston Hill, but it may be a few feet higher somewhere in the woods to the west. The ridge runs almost immediately into Hertfordshire and within a mile comes the summit of this county also—Point 802, close to Hastoe. At Tring yet another spillway gap is traversed by the Grand Union Canal, the Midland Region main line and the A41 trunk road.

From here the scarp line runs north for 4 miles to Ivinghoe Beacon. The Ashridge Estate above, owned by the National Trust, comprises more than 6 square miles of wood, heath and down; below is the conical chalk outlier of Pitstone Hill. The slopes are steep at Ivinghoe and there is a summit camp. Now too, says Massingham, the scenery is different:

> The conical shapes of the hills and the indented line of the ridge from Pitstone Hill to the beacon and again along Five Knolls Hill overlooking Dunstable are curious rather than beautiful. But they are much nearer primordial downland in appearance, though nothing like so grand in mass, height or contour as the inspired lines of the chalk in Wiltshire, Berkshire and the South.

Two miles ahead is Whipsnade Zoo, the site marked by the white figure of a lion cut on the hill side. The pens are spacious and verdant; the animals, however, seem to have developed the knack of lurking in the centres as far away as possible from curious eyes. Nearby circle and swoop the sail planes of the London Gliding Club. Point 798 on the road running along the top of Dunstable Downs is the county summit of Bedfordshire.

At this point we are some 25 crow-flight miles from Shirburn Hill, the county summit of Oxfordshire, having passed over those of Buckinghamshire and Hertfordshire *en route*. This suggests another purposive walk in the South East, well within the powers of the average walker. The highest points of all the counties of England and Wales were listed by E. Moss in the *Rucksack Club Journal* in 1951. At the time of writing he had already visited all of them; I have not heard of anyone else doing it since. The selection is usually obvious in hilly counties but there are difficulties in the case of very flat areas, thus the Holland Division of Lincoln with a highest point of 25 ft had to be referred to the Ordnance Survey. Through accident of site and boundary many hills, prominent and well known, do not appear, for example Butser Hill in the South Downs, Inkpen Hill etc. The flat-topped chalk downs also present problems, for successive hills often differ in height by only a few feet, with the highest in no way prominent—see, for example, Betsom's Hill, the county summit of Kent. Any hill under 1,000 ft may have cultivation running over the top and thus be difficult of access, as Moss says of one of them:

> When I visited it in August 1937, the summit was covered by a cornfield, which had fortunately been cut, though the stooks were still there. Had the corn been standing, I wonder whether I would have had the temerity to wade through it.

And of another:

I hesitate to describe in print how I succeeded in reaching the highest point.

The other summit-collecting mania which afflicts some climbers is the ascent of all peaks on certain lists, such as the 2,000 ft mountains of England and Wales, the 3,000 ft mountains of Scotland, and so on. Nothing like this has yet hit the South East, but it is conceivable that to reach every 800 ft hill within 80 miles of London would be a task of some magnitude and very full of scenic interest.

A mile or two to the north the Chilterns end abruptly at Dunstable. Close by there is a fort on an outlier at Totternhoe. The stone for Windsor Castle came from the quarries here and there was also a chalk mine similar to that at Chislehurst. This was described by a Swedish traveller, Pehr Kalm, in 1748:

> The adits into the chalk hill went mostly horizontally, yet they sloped a little down in some places. On both sides of the main adits there were other adits both *ad angulos acutos, rectos et obtusos*, so that if the entrances of all these cross galleries had been open this would have been to one unacquainted with them the worst labyrinth and maze there could possibly be.

In the 1930s Arthur Bonner told how he had entered this series in 1915, but there seems to be no record of access in recent years.

Before setting out on the final lap into East Anglia, and henceforward there is no high continuous ridge to look forward to, we look back at a few isolated hills which rise from the plain to the north. The hills at Muswell and Brill on the Buckingham–Oxford border are over 600 ft; the village of Brill planted squarely on the summit has tremendous views in all directions. Eight miles northeast Quainton Hill is also over 600 ft. The Lower Greensand makes a brief appearance north of Leighton Buzzard, continuing to the north-east as far as Sandy and Potton. The highest point, just over 550 ft, is close to Woburn Sands.

Beyond Dunstable and Luton there is no continuous interest for the walker. The Barton Hills a few miles north of the latter, which reach over 600 ft, have the Icknield Way traversing their southern flanks. The chalk country rolls on towards Cambridge. The highest points of that county (478 ft) and of Essex (458 ft) are only $1\frac{1}{2}$ miles apart near Great Chishill. The Gog-Magog Hills, one time site of another chalk giant, project into the plain towards the City of Cambridge, which has, we shall find, figured largely in the story of minor climbing.

The exploits of university mountaineers in the chalk pits at Cherryhinton, 2 miles south-east of Cambridge, were first described in a note by Ivan Waller in *Cambridge Mountaineering*, 1925–6. The rock of course was of poor quality and loose:

> An axe of some sort is essential, not only for cutting steps, but also for clearing away the looser chalk on the surface. The hands have to rely almost entirely on push supports, and progress upwards or downwards must be made by the feet.

He indicated the whereabouts of various routes, adding, 'minute details would be superfluous as the climbs have a habit of disappearing overnight'! Apart from the natural rock some climbs were made also on two disused kilns in one of the quarries.

In 1934 E. J. C. Kendall contributed a much longer account to the same journal, summing up the facilities as follows:

> It is climbing in miniature, but within their modest height the climbs contain a surprising variety of problems, and they give on a small scale practice in many departments of mountaineering. It is not mere freak climbing, bouldering on peculiar rocks; indeed, it can teach a good deal in the way of balance technique. Rush and grab methods simply will not work on a rock of extremely variable quality; for even at its best each hold needs testing, and the climber will do well to maintain as many points of attachment as possible.

As the quarries were still being worked the routes were continually changing—'new routes are constantly made from the ruins of the old'; nevertheless he thought it well worthwhile to describe some of them in detail.

The quarries themselves have not been the subject of any subsequent literature, but the so-called Cherryhinton Wall, probably that suggested by Waller for abseil practice, was described in *Cambridge Mountaineering* in 1965. This brick wall in one of the quarries was once the retaining wall to a limekiln. There are nine obvious routes and several variations; the height is about 30 ft. All this serves to show what can be done with walls and chalk pits by climbers who are sufficiently desperate; it is certain that a great deal more of this sort of thing is done than ever gets into print.

Some of the earliest sporting climbs on buildings were on the walls and roofs of the Cambridge colleges, at any rate it was Cambridge that produced the first specific literature. Geoffrey Winthrop Young was the pioneer with *A Roof Climber's Guide to Trinity* in 1900—'a practical description', he claimed, 'of all Routes'. Here is his nocturnal climbing scenery:

> The distant towers looming against the dark sky, lit by the flickering lamps far below; the gradations of light and shadow, marked by an occasional moving black speck seemingly in another world; the sheer wall descending into darkness at his side, above which he has been half suspended on his long ascent, the almost invisible barrier that the battlements from which he started seem to make to his terminating in the Cloisters if his arm slips, all contribute to making this deservedly-esteemed the finest view point in the College Alps.

Young's treatise on the sport, *Wall and Roof Climbing*, appeared six years later—an erudite and fanciful history backed by extensive quotation, with a background of commentary on every aspect, for instance the comparison with rock climbing:

> The great feature which distinguishes roof climbing from rock climbing and renders its pursuit difficult, not only for the beginner but even for the mountain expert, lies in the abruptness of the angles. Even in the Dolomites, whose ledge and chimney effects most closely resemble the straight-line architecture of the builders' ideal, vertical walls are rare, and generally permit of evasion or relentingly disclose some vulnerable crack. But the builder exults to show his superiority to Nature and his contempt for her soft-hearted methods. His walls are as straight as plumb-line can make them, his tiled or slated gables maliciously turn all their holds the wrong way, his chimney-stacks emulate the intellectual development of the early Victorian high hat. Wonderful is the difference two or three degrees make in the rapidity and security of the young climber's progress. . . . There is a curious parallelism between rock and roof which will enable many a difficult problem to be solved by analogy.

A notable event between the wars was the publication of *The Night Climbers of Cambridge* by the anonymous Whipplesnaith, a full-scale account, liberally illustrated with flash-light photographs. Climbs were described in narrative form on five of the colleges, as well as on other university buildings, and intensely readable and exciting it certainly is. Cambridge, says the author, means different things to different people. To us it brings back 'a jumble of pipes and chimneys and pinnacles, leading up from security to adventure'. The roof climber has twin excitements—the climb itself and the possibility of being caught in an activity absolutely forbidden by the authorities, for which the penalties are severe. The sport is only possible in a place like a university where a range of buildings, preferably of more ancient architectural types, fall under one authority. In more public situations it would be difficult to avoid confusion with cat burglary. The climbing must be carried out, therefore, in darkness, which, depending on the individual, may lessen or heighten the sensation of the moves. Records are few and climbers, at least in their active years, anonymous.

A guidebook to the roofs of St John's was published between the wars as was a second edition of the Trinity volume (1960 saw a third edition). Techniques remain much the same even though standards of achievement are advancing:

> The tricky part is at the top; the pipe stops short of the battle-ments. When he reaches the bowl, the climber must raise his body until his chest is level with his hands, then thrust his right hand deep into a drainage hole just above the bowl, to find an undercut finger hold. The left knee finds a resting place on a small sloping ledge and the left hand reaches out quickly, high and wide, to grasp the embrasure of the battlements. The right hand joins the left; a pull-up brings the feet to the bowl; and the last step is easy.

Because of these literary associations, we have lingered over the climbing in Cambridge; in fact other buildings in other places are sometimes climbed for sport and not felony. We shall never know about most of them and, if moved to participate, are unlikely in our turn to leave records.

Back on the hills again we continue north-eastwards to New-market, beyond which the chalk is overlain with sands to form the heathy area known as Breckland. There are new state forests here, while Thetford has one of the biggest castle mounds in the country. Near Brandon are Grime's Graves, the flint mines for which the prehistoric travellers made their long journeys on these chalk hills from Salisbury Plain. The site was excavated in the last century and two shafts have been left open for us to see how the diminutive miners lived and worked. Eventually the chalk reappears in the cliffs at Hunstanton.

The Great Ridgeway and its extensions would make a magnifi-cent long-distance route, which might well be designated with rights-of-way over the whole length some time in the future. From the coast at Axmouth in Devon it is some 240 miles to Grime's Graves in Norfolk and some 275 miles to the sea's edge beside the Wash. The whole range of England's history can be seen by the way.

APPENDICES

APPENDIX A

THE 120-MILE CIRCLE

WITHIN the preceding chapters I have dealt with that area of the South East which is comfortably accessible to the Londoner in day trips, namely that within a radius of about 80 miles. In this appendix the treatment is extended to cover an area suitable for a weekend or overnight trip, assumed to lie within a radius of about 120 miles. This brings within reach a whole range of interesting rock types and structures—the exciting combination of Purbeck Limestone and sea cliffs in Dorset, the great Mountain Limestone crags of the gorges and sea coast of Somerset, the Oolitic Limestone range of the Cotswolds with a few short climbable rock walls, sandstone in the Forest of Dean, Mountain Limestone again in the lower Wye Valley, sandstone again in Worcestershire, ancient igneous rocks at Malvern and farther northwards and eastwards in Charnwood Forest, gritstone in Staffordshire and a length of lovely coastline round the bulge of north Norfolk, where the sea cliffs are, unfortunately, uselessly crumbly. This diversity adds a great deal of variety to the south-eastern climbing scene and is in fact firmly a part of it. Then finally we have many miles of cliffy coastline on the far side of the Channel. (For Refs, see p 154.)

*　　*　　*

THE DORSET COAST (SWANAGE TO PORTLAND)

The climbing is on a limestone, the Purbeck, which is yellow rather than the usual grey. Some of the routes are on quarried faces usually up to about 30 ft, but most are on natural cliffs and reach as much as 120 ft in places. The coastline is formed in gently curving lines with no large bays or indentations; there is no foreshore or backshore, but the climbs start from block ledges at the foot which have often to be reached by abseil. The tidal range is small and it is the height of the waves which constitutes the main sea hazard.

The principal crags lie in the 5 miles between Durlston Head and St Aldhelm's Head. Access is limited, or even barred altogether to some parts near Tilly Whim. More climbs have been made near Lulworth Cove and Durdle Door, also in Portland. There are chalk climbing possibilities also.

Fine walking is available on the South-West Peninsula Coast Path, which traverses this clifftop all the way, except for a diversion round the ranges between Kimmeridge and Lulworth. The ridge of the Purbeck Hills is also worthy.

Road miles from London: Swanage 123, Lulworth 122, Weymouth 132.

Refs: Pyatt (1968); White (1969).

THE MENDIP HILLS

The rock is Mountain Limestone exposed in fine natural crags up to 400 ft high which give rock scenery as impressive as anywhere in the country. Both the major sites in the big gorges are exposed to public view; there will probably be spectators and from time to time threats of closure in the public interest. Standards are high.

The crags in the gorges of Cheddar (televised in 1965) and Avon (within the bounds of the City of Bristol) are outstanding; those in Ebbor Gorge, at Churchill, on Brean Down and Middle Hope are lesser; there are some quarries also.

This is a major caving area with Swildon's Hole as long, deep, complex and full of problems as any in the country. There are many more caves, large and small, of all standards and it is possible to work one's way through expeditions of ever-increasing difficulty.

The hills, their scarp facing south-west, do not provide an outstanding ridge walk, but the flatness of the plains below accentuates the height. The summit is Black Down (1,067 ft).

Road miles from London: Bristol 116, Shepton Mallet 118, Wells 122, Cheddar 130, Weston-super-Mare 136.

Refs: Barrington (1964); Dixon (1964); Drummond (1967); Pyatt (1968).

THE COTSWOLD HILLS

The rock is Oolitic Limestone, a famous building stone, of which there are unfortunately only a few small outcrops and quarries up to 30 ft high. The best of these are Castle Rock on Cleeve Hill, Crickley Hill, Haresfield Beacon, Randwick Quarry and the Devil's

Chimney on Leckhampton Hill. There are other quarries further south towards Bristol.

The scarp slope of these hills demarcates the Severn Valley. The summit is Cleeve Hill (1,082 ft); Broadway Hill further north is the nearest 1,000 ft point to London; the hill line continues on into Northamptonshire. As walking country the main interest lies perhaps in the works of man rather than in nature.

Road miles from London: Broadway 92, Cheltenham 98.

Refs: Calvert (1958); Anon (Gloucestershire MC 1965).

THE FOREST OF DEAN

Climbing on rock described as 'a rather friable and sandy cement containing a vast number of quartz pebbles' has been done on sites at Wigpool Common, Hope Mansel, Plump Hill, Parkend, Hacker's Cutting and Staple Edge. There is a notable large boulder —the Suckstone. Nothing exceeds 30 ft.

This is one of the largest of our National Forest Parks.

Road miles from London: Coleford 124.

Ref: Calvert (1958).

THE LOWER WYE VALLEY

This is another magnificent Mountain Limestone area with huge crags at Wintour's Leap, $1\frac{1}{2}$ miles above Chepstow, and on either side of the River by Symond's Yat. Routes up to 200 ft are available, also pinnacles only attainable by climbing.

Road miles from London: Symond's Yat 127, Chepstow 128.

Refs: Calvert (1958); Anon (Gloucestershire MC 1965).

THE MALVERN HILLS

This 9-mile miniature mountain range in very ancient rocks reaches 1,394 ft at the Worcestershire Beacon above Malvern. There are spacious views on every hand from the summit ridge.

Natural outcrops provide short climbs here and there; various quarries on North Hill have also been used. Hardly worth travelling any distance for, but quite interesting if you happen to be there.

Road miles from London: Great Malvern 119.

Ref: There is no guidebook, the only account is in the *MAM Journal*, 1951.

WORCESTERSHIRE SANDSTONE

There are isolated outcrops of sandstone in Worcestershire which have been used by climbers. In the Habberley Valley near Kidderminster are some short rock walls and an isolated pinnacle; there are short rock walls too on the north-west side of the ridge of Kinver Edge. The rock appears again beside the River Severn north of Bewdley, where two long routes were recorded in 1967.

Road miles from London: Kidderminster 122, Bewdley 125.

Refs: No guidebook. See *Climbers' Club Journal* 1928 and *New Climbs* (Climbers' Club, 1968).

CHARNWOOD FOREST

This is an upland area of ancient igneous rocks in Leicestershire which reaches 912 ft at Bardon Hill. The chief natural outcrop—the 30 ft Hangingstone Rocks near Woodhouse Eaves—is not readily accessible. Longer climbs have been done in quarries nearby and at Bardon Quarry. Lesser rocks are found at Beacon Hill, Bradgate Park, Whitwick, Hawcliffe Hill, Craig Buddon, Blackbrook Reservoir, High Sharpley, Ives Head and elsewhere.

Road miles from London: 105.

Ref: Vickers (nd).

THE QUARRY AREA OF SOUTH WEST LEICESTERSHIRE

The rock is Diorite and quarries near Enderby and Huncote give routes of 150 ft or so—an important modern discovery.

Road miles from London: 95.

Ref: Vickers (nd).

TWO CLASSIC MIDLAND SITES

The Dolomite Limestone quarries at Breedon-on-the-Hill once 150 ft high have been quarried away. At the turn of the century E. A. Baker could write:

> Anyone familiar with mountain scenery cannot fail to be charmed with the mimic precipices, peaks and chasms of Breedon; but the place has a beauty quite its own if seen when the crags are all ablaze with wall-flowers and gorgeous tufts of snapdragon, creamy and purple, and many a flower known only to the botanist, growing where there is no hand to pluck.

The Hemlock Stone, a 30 ft sandstone pinnacle at Nottingham, is now fenced off. In the same period the same author found sport on it:

. . . now the leader leans outwards and feels for handhold. For a moment his feet continue to graze the rock, while he gropes about for something trusty to clutch; then he lays hold higher up, his body swings out, and now he must pull up with might and main over the rugosities of the roof.

THE NORFOLK COAST

There is no sport here for the coasteer, nevertheless this coastline of sea cliffs in the newest of young rocks, of salt marshes and sands, of erosion and deposition, provides considerable variety for the walker. The main sea cliffs are close to Hunstanton and further east between Weybourne and Happisburgh, reaching over 200 ft in the neighbourhood of Cromer.

Road miles from London: Hunstanton 114, Cromer 133.

THE COAST OF NORTHERN FRANCE
(CALAIS TO ÉTRETAT)

This coastal strip falls surprisingly within a 120-mile circle of London. A considerable amount of climbing has been done on chalk, of particular interest to us because of the untapped prospects of chalk on this side of the Channel. Étretat, 16 miles from Le Havre, is the main site with three headlands terminating in impressive arches—the Manneport (which would, it is said, give passage to a ship with all sails flying), the Porte d'Aval ('an elephant plunging his trunk into the sea') and the Porte d'Amont. These cliffs are well over 200 ft high. Off the Porte d'Aval rises a 260 ft pinnacle—l'Aiguillette—which has been linked with the headland by a Tyrolean traverse. Many routes have been done hereabouts mostly requiring artificial techniques.

There are other spectacular chalk cliffs further along the coast towards Dieppe; indeed a walk on the clifftop from Le Havre to Dieppe would be a most interesting expedition of about 70 miles.

A climb has also been made on Cap Blanc Nez near Calais, where the chalk cliffs reach more than 400 ft. Again artificial techniques were used on a material more akin to English chalk than that found further west.

Access: By sea crossing Southampton–Le Havre $6\frac{1}{2}$–$8\frac{1}{2}$ hours; Newhaven–Dieppe $3\frac{1}{2}$–4 hours; Dover–Calais $1\frac{1}{2}$ hours. By air crossing Southend–Calais 30 minutes.

Ref: Bocianowski (1965).

I

FURTHER AFIELD IN BRITAIN

WE turn finally to climbing areas even further from the South East, that is to say beyond the 120-mile radius of the previous appendix, but which are nevertheless reasonably accessible for week-end trips because of the excellence of the communications. The importance of this more distant climbing relative to purely local activities has increased considerably in recent years. Whereas week-end climbing thirty years ago was confined almost entirely to a circle of 60–80 miles radius and climbing practice was contrived therein against the time when there was opportunity to travel further afield, nowadays it has become commonplace to journey as far as North Wales, South Wales, Devonshire, and so on. A whole range of rock types is available from the rhyolite and granite of our hills and mountains through to limestone, gritstone and sandstone exposed in crag face, outcrop, quarry or sea cliff. The continuous development of motorways and the post-steam speeding up of railway services is going to make these far-off rocks even more important in the future.

*   *   *

SOUTH DEVON

A considerable amount of climbing is available nowadays in the Torbay area, the principal sites being Chudleigh Rocks, Berry Head, Meadfoot Quarry, Telegraph Hole Quarry and Daddyhole (Torquay), the cliffs between Oddicombe Bay and Anstey's Cove and Galmpton Quarry. The rock is Devonian Limestone. Standards are very high, particularly at Berry Head.

There are caves also.

Road miles from London: Chudleigh 178, Torquay 191.

Rail access: Torquay is only $3\frac{1}{2}$–4 hours from Paddington.

Refs: Moulton (1966), *New Climbs* (Climbers' Club, 1968), Pyatt (1968).

DARTMOOR

This moorland block, the principal granite mass of the West Country, reaches 2,038 ft at High Willhays. It is fine mountain-type walking country where map and compass are indispensable; a north to south crossing makes a worthy expedition.

The crags on the moor are all granite, those round the edges are sometimes shales. On the east side and most accessible from the South East are Hay Tor, Hound Tor, Greator Rocks and Bowerman's Nose on the Moor, and Lustleigh Cleave, Sharp Tor, Blackingstone Rock and Heltor outside it.

The finest rock exposures—Dewer Stone, Sheep's Tor and Morwell Rocks—are on the south-west side and relatively inaccessible.

Road miles from London: Moretonhampstead 183, Okehampton 193.

Refs: Moulton (1966), Pyatt (1968).

NORTH DEVON AND EXMOOR

This is a fine walking area with the moor peaking at 1,705 ft at Dunkery Beacon and a splendid section of the South-West Peninsula Coast Path running along hills of over 1,000 ft adjacent to the coastline.

There are two sea cliff areas offering contrasting climbing. The coast from County Gate to Saunton Sands has been traversed at the cliff foot; the cliffs are high and steep, easy ways down are few, so that the tidal range of 25 ft constitutes a major problem. The rocks are Devonian slates and sandstones.

Beyond the Taw–Torridge Estuary the shales and sandstones of the Culm Measures form savage cliffs between Clovelly and Widemouth. Several straightforward routes have been made, others await.

Road miles from London: Minehead 169, Lynmouth 186, Ilfracombe 203, Clovelly 215, Bude 220.

Refs: Archer (1961–5); Moulton (1966); Pyatt (1968).

SOUTH WALES

In those parts of South Wales nearest to the South East there are numerous interesting mountain groups but only a little rock climbing. The nearest 2,000 ft mountain to London, a nameless point (2,003 ft) on a ridge between the valleys of Olechon and Ewyas, is in the Black Mountains, which reach 2,660 ft at Waun Fach. To the south beyond the Usk there are limestone climbs and extensive caves at Llangattock.

On westwards the Brecon Beacons rise to 2,906 ft. Some climbing

has been done on the northern scarp at times when frost and ice
have bound together the loose rocks.

Further north in Radnorshire is Radnor Forest (Great Rhos,
2,166 ft), a moorland block without rocks. There are some scanty
outcrops in the surrounding countryside.

Road miles from London: Abergavenny 144, Crickhowell 150,
New Radnor 159, Talgarth 161, Brecon 164.

Refs: There are no climbers' guides at present. We are promised
something in due course by the Climbers' Club.

NORTH WALES

Weekend trips to North Wales are very popular nowadays with
London climbers. There is an extensive range of mountain crags
and climbing of all standards of difficulty. There are also the large
outcrop type crags at Tremadoc and the sea cliffs at Holyhead, the
latter considerably further from London however than the comparable cliffs at Berry Head, for example.

The Welsh 3,000s, a walkers' route visiting the fourteen summits
above 3,000 ft in Snowdonia, is also possible in a weekend with
appropriate organisation. The 30 miles and 18,000 ft of ascent and
descent have been done in just under $5\frac{1}{2}$ hours.

Road miles from London: Pen y Gwryd 224 (said to have been
done once in 2 hours and 57 minutes), Tremadoc 225, Holyhead
259.

Refs: The Climbers' Club series of guidebooks.

THE LAKE DISTRICT

The Lake District is much farther from London, though eventually the M1/M6 combination may make the journey straightforward enough. As the classic crags on the far side of the mountain
block involve quite long detours even when you get there, it is not
really suited for weekend trips.

Road miles from London: Ambleside 267.

Refs: The Fell and Rock Climbing Club series of guidebooks.

THE PEAK DISTRICT

The nearest classical climbing ground to the South East is in
the Peak District National Park. This comprises two contrasting
districts: the White (Low) Peak in the south is limestone country
with gritstone edges along either side, the Black (High) Peak in the

north is high moorland capped with gritstone having limestone in the valleys. There are considerable amounts of outcropping rock giving gritstone climbing, greatly contrasting limestone climbing and an extensive caving area, where the natural caverns form a honeycomb with old mine workings.

On the high northern peat moors there is a long tradition of hard walking, centred mainly on Manchester.

Road miles from London: Matlock 143, Dovedale 143, Buxton 159, Sheffield 160, Manchester 184.

Refs: There have been several series of guidebooks. The next is to be published by the Climbers' Club.

APPENDIX C

FURTHER AFIELD ON THE CONTINENT

THE chalk climbing on the north coast of France, described in Appendix B, could reasonably be reached on foot from the Channel ports. I deal here finally with certain Continental sites which require a car for access; even so these may be regarded as part of the amenities of the South East. Climbers living on the side of London nearest to the Continent, whose journey to home mountains has to begin with a traverse of the traffic of the capital, have considerable incentive to go towards these cross-Channel sites. (Southend is 264 miles from North Wales, but only 45 minutes flying plus 110 road miles from Freyr in the Ardennes.)

THE SEINE VALLEY

In the valley of the Seine between Mantes and just below Rouen various chalk cliffs have yielded extensive climbing during the last decade. The most developed is that on the right bank between Connelles and Amfreville where there are 200 routes up to 150 ft long. Other important sites are between Les Andelys and Le Roque, at La Roche Guyon by Mantes and at Rochers d'Orival, la Bouille, la Fontaine and Jumieges, all close to Rouen.

Access—Sea crossings: Newhaven–Dieppe and Southampton–Le Havre. Dieppe–Connelles 55 miles, Le Havre–Connelles 75 miles.

Ref: Bocianowski (1965).

FONTAINEBLEAU

West of the town in the triangle Melun, Nemours, Étampes, there are extensive outcrops of sandstone which would look very familiar to the Tunbridge Wells enthusiast. There are many crags scattered over a wide area, the highest 45 ft, very popular with Parisian climbers. It is perhaps rather a long way to go for what there is when you get there.

Access—Sea crossing: Newhaven–Dieppe. Dieppe–Fontainebleau 146 miles.

Ref: Anon (CIM de la FSGT 1967).

A candid view of Fontainebleau (and perhaps of Tunbridge Wells also) *Piero Rossi*

THE BELGIAN ARDENNES

There is a magnificent limestone climbing area here centred on a 25-mile stretch of the River Meuse between Waulsort above Dinant and Marche-les-Dames downstream from Namur. The best known crag site is at Freyr, 4½ miles above Dinant, where there are 250 routes up to 400 ft. Other important crags are the Rochers de Champalle at Yvoir, the Rochers de Neviou at Dave and Marche-les-Dames beyond Namur.

There are a few rocks even nearer to England, around Charleroi, and a great many more beyond the main area south of Liège.

Access—Sea crossing: Dover–Ostende.

Air crossing: Southend or Lydd–Ostende.

From Ostende—Charleroi 100 miles, Namur 110 miles, Liège 130 miles.

Ref: Anon (Club Alpin Belge, 1966).

SWITZERLAND

In conclusion it is interesting to examine briefly the possibility of climbing a real mountain in a weekend from London. It seems possible to leave London on Friday evening and reach Zermatt by air and rail in time for breakfast on Saturday; the return journey starting late on Sunday afternoon will land our hypothetical traveller back in London just before midnight. Some thirty hours are thus available to climb one of the local peaks and it is thus theoretically possible. The expense would be formidable, as would the problem of rapid acclimatisation; the weather risk would be considerable, though it might be minimised by careful study of forecasts.

Other valleys and their mountains might well be equally difficult of access, as well as equally interesting to reach.

BIBLIOGRAPHY

GENERAL

Anon. *An Account of the Principal Pleasure Tours in England and Wales.* 1822
Anon. *Guide to all the Watering and Sea Bathing Places.* 1826
Camden, William. *Brittania.* Original in Latin, 1586; translation into English by Philemon Holland, 1610; several subsequent editions
Cobbett, William. *Rural Rides,* 1821–32
Cochrane, C. *The Lost Roads of Wessex.* David & Charles, 1969
Cox, R. Hippisley. *The Green Roads of England.* Methuen, 1934
Davies, G. M. *The Geology of London and South East England.* Murby, 1939
Defoe, Daniel. *A Tour through Great Britain.* 1724–26
Drayton, Michael. *Polyolbion.* 1613–22
Harper, C. G. and Kershaw, J. C. *The Downs and the Sea.* Palmer, 1923
Leland, John. *The Itinerary of John Leland in or about the years 1535–1543.* First published 1710. Centaur Press 1964
Marples, M. *White Horses and other Hill Figures.* Country Life, 1949
Massingham, H. J. *English Downland.* Batsford, 1936, 1949
Timperley, H. W. and Brill, E. *Ancient Trackways of Wessex.* Phoenix, 1965
Topley, W. *The Geology of the Weald.* Geological Survey, 1875
Walpole, G. A. *New British Traveller.* 1784
Wooldridge, S. W. and Goldring, F. *The Weald.* Collins, 1953
Wooldridge, S. W. and Hutchings, G. E. *London's Countryside.* Methuen, 1964

CHAPTER 1.   NORTH DOWNS AND GREENSANDS

Belloc, Hilaire. *The Old Road.* Constable, 1904
Goodsall, R. H. *The Ancient Road to Canterbury.* Constable, 1960
Green, F. E. *The Surrey Hills.* Chatto & Windus, 1915
Henderson J., Hillman, B. and Pearman, H. *More Secret Tunnels in Surrey.* Chelsea Speleological Society, 1968
Pearman, H. *Dene Holes.* Chelsea Speleological Society, 1966
Pearman, H. *Secret Tunnels in Surrey.* Chelsea Speleological Society, 1963

CHAPTER 2.   SOUTH DOWNS AND NEIGHBOURING HILLS

Belloc, Hilaire. *The Stane Street.* Constable, 1913

Green, E. G. *The South Downs Way*. Ramblers' Association, 1968
Harrison, D. *Along the South Downs*. Cassell, 1958
Matthews, E. C. *The Highlands of South West Surrey*. Black, 1911
Straker, E. *Wealden Iron*. Bell, 1911 (reprinted David & Charles, 1968)
White, Gilbert. *The Natural History of Selborne*. 1789 (many subsequent editions)
Winbolt, S. E. *With a Spade on Stane Street*. Methuen, 1936

CHAPTER 3. SANDSTONE CLIMBS

Bryson, H. Courtney. *Rock Climbs round London*. Privately pub, 1936
Pyatt, Edward C. *Sandstone Climbs in South East England*. Privately pub, 1947
Pyatt, Edward C. *South East England*. Climbers' Club, 1956 (revised 1963—by D. G. Fagan, J. V. Smoker and Edward C. Pyatt; revised 1969—by L. R. and L. E. Holliwell)
Sheffield, M. O. and Bryson, H. Courtney. *Guide to the Climbs at Harrison's Rocks near Groombridge*. Privately pub, 1934

CHAPTER 4. COASTEERING IN THE SOUTH EAST

Bullock, H. Somerset. 'Chalk Climbing on Beachy Head.' *Climbers' Club Journal*, February, 1899
Crowley, E. A. 'Chalk Climbing on Beachy Head.' *Scottish Mountaineering Club Journal*, May, 1895
de Selincourt, A. *The Channel Shore*. Hale, 1953
Harper, C. G. *The Kentish Coast*. Chapman & Hall, 1914
Haskett Smith, W. P. *Rock Climbing in the British Isles—England*. Longmans Green, 1894
Murray, J. W. C. *Romney Marsh*. Hale, 1953
Steers, J. A. *The Coastline of England and Wales*. Cambridge, 1947

CHAPTER 5. SOLENT SHORES

Edlin, H. L. (ed) *The New Forest* (Forestry Commission Guide). HMSO, 1961
Phillips-Birt, D. *Waters of Wight*. Cassell, 1967
Wightman, R. *The Wessex Heathlands*. Hale, 1954
Wilson, L. *Portrait of the Isle of Wight*. Hale, 1965

CHAPTER 6. SALISBURY PLAIN

Timperley, H. W. *The Vale of Pewsey*. Hale, 1954
Whitlock, R. *Salisbury Plain*. Hale, 1955

CHAPTER 7. THE GREAT RIDGEWAY

Anon. *Roof Climbers' Guide to St John's*. Metcalfe, 1921
Anon. *The Night Climber's Guide to Trinity*. Weatherhead, 1960

Massingham, H. J. *Chiltern Country*. Batsford, 1940

Whipplesnaith. *The Night Climbers of Cambridge*. Chatto & Windus, 1937

Young, G. Winthrop. *Roof Climbers' Guide to Trinity*. Spalding, 1900

Young, G. Winthrop. *Wall and Roof Climbing*. Spottiswoode, 1905.

APPENDICES

Anon. *Guide des Rochers Belges et Luxembourgeois*. Club Alpin Belge, 1966

Anon. *Rock Climbs in the Wye Valley and the Cotswolds*. Gloucestershire Mountaineering Club, 1965

Anon. *South Devon Climbing Guide*. Exeter MC, in preparation

Anon. *Topo-Guide des Groupes de Rochers d'Escalade des Massifs Greseux de Fontainebleau* CIM de la FSGT, Paris, 1967

Archer, C. H. *Coastal Climbs in North Devon*, with supplements. Privately pub, 1961–5

Barrington, N. *The Caves of Mendip. Dalesman*, 1964

Bocianowski, F. *Falaises de la Seine—Connelles*. Section Montagne du RSCM, 1965

Calvert, F. T. (ed). *Some Gloucestershire Climbs*. Gloucestershire Mountaineering Club, 1958

Dixon, J. *Limestone Climbs in South West England*. Limestone Climbing Group, 1964

Drummond, E. Ward. *Extremely Severe in Avon Gorge*. Privately pub, 1967

Moulton, R. D. (ed). *Rock Climbing in Devonshire*. Royal Navy Mountaineering Club, 1966

Pyatt, Edward C. *A Climber in the West Country*. David & Charles, 1968

Vickers, K. S. *Rock Climbs in Leicestershire*. Leicester Association of Mountaineers, nd

White, R. C. (ed). *Dorset*. Climbers' Club, 1969

LIST OF CLUBS AND ORGANISATIONS

Countryside Commission, 1 Cambridge Gate, London, NW1

Formerly the National Parks Commission. A government body set up under the National Parks and Access to the Countryside Act, 1949. Administers in south-east England;

(a) Areas of Outstanding Natural Beauty—The Isle of Wight (73 square miles), Surrey Hills (160 square miles), East Hampshire (151 square miles), Chichester Harbour (29 square miles).

(b) The South Downs Way.

National Trust, 42 Queen Anne's Gate, London, SW1

A private organisation formed in 1895 and financed by endowments, legacies, donations and subscriptions. Owns approximately 90 square miles in the 80-mile circle round London, including, for example, Frencham Ponds and Common, the Devil's Jumps, the Devil's Punchbowl and Gibbet Hill, Selborne Hill, Cissbury Ring, Ditchling Beacon, Combe Hill, Leith Hill, Box Hill, Black Down, etc.

Forestry Commission, 25 Savile Row, London, W1

A government body, founded in 1919, now a very considerable landowner in the country as a whole. Its chief interests in the South East are the New Forest and the forests of Breckland, but there are numerous smaller holdings all over the area.

Nature Conservancy, 19 Belgrave Square, London, SW1

The government conservation body. Protects numerous national nature reserves in the South East, including Old Winchester Hill, Fyfield Down, etc.

Royal Society for the Protection of Birds, The Lodge, Sandy, Beds.

A private conservation organisation which administers a number of sites in the South East, including Dungeness, etc.

Society for the Promotion of Nature Reserves, British Museum (Natural History), Cromwell Road, London, SW7

The society owns nature reserves and co-ordinates the work of the county naturalists' trusts. For the South East these are the Naturalists' Trusts for Bedfordshire and Huntingdonshire; Berkshire, Buckinghamshire and Oxfordshire; Cambridge and Isle of Ely; Essex; Hampshire and Isle of Wight; Kent; Suffolk; Surrey; and Sussex. There is also the Hertfordshire and Middlesex Trust for Nature Conservation.

Council for the Preservation of Rural England, 4 Hobart Place, London, SW1

Ramblers' Association, 124 Finchley Road, London, NW3

CLIMBING CLUBS IN THE SOUTH EAST

Aldermaston Mountaineering Club, The Alpine Club, Aylesbury Climbing Club, British Petroleum Mountaineering Club, Cambridge Mountaineering Club, Dunstable and District Mountaineering Club, Harrow Mountaineering Club, Junior Mountaineering Club of Scotland (London Section), London Mountaineering Club, North London Mountaineering Club, Oxford Mountaineering Club, Peterborough Mountaineering Club, Reading Mountaineering Club, Rockhoppers (South West London Mountaineering Club), RAE Mountaineering Club, Rugby Mountaineering Club, Sandstone Climbing Club, South Essex Climbing Club, Southern Mountaineering Association, Tuesday Climbing Club, Wellingborough Mountaineering Club, Wessex Mountaineering Club, Yeti Club (London Section).

There are clubs at the Universities of Cambridge, East Anglia, London, Oxford, Reading, and Southampton; at some of the component colleges of London University; at the Royal Military Academy Sandhurst and at many lesser educational establishments. There are clubs too at some of the London hospitals.

Current addresses can be obtained from the British Mountaineering Council.

ACKNOWLEDGEMENTS

THIS book owes much to my many friends, mostly London members of the Junior Mountaineering Club of Scotland, who climbed, walked and caved with me in the South East over a period of many active years. We looked out on the good things of climbing spread, too widely it seemed, around us; we accepted and made the most of this pattern imposed on our climbing lives and then enjoyed ourselves hugely. In those early days we tried to think of, and to use, London as an all-the-year-round climbing centre; now with increased leisure and improved transport it is firmly established in just that role.

Acknowledgment is made to the following for permission to quote from the journals and books listed:

Methuen & Co Ltd for *Mountain Craft* by G. Winthrop Young; Chapman & Hall Ltd for *Caving* by E. A. Baker; B. T. Batsford Ltd for *English Downland* and *Chiltern Country* by H. J. Massingham; Robert Hale & Co for *Portrait of the Isle of Wight* by L. Wilson; The Hamlyn Publishing Group Ltd for *English Excursions* by G. Grigson; A. D. Peters & Co for *The Old Road* by Hilaire Belloc; Laurence Pollinger Ltd for *Salisbury Plain* by R. Whitlock; Macmillan & Co Ltd for *Highways and Byways in Sussex* by E. V. Lucas; Christy & Moore Ltd for *The Spirit of the Hills* by F. S. Smythe; Andrew Young for his *English Excursions*; R. H. A. Staniforth for personal correspondence; the editors of the *Alpine Journal* and the *Scottish Mountaineering Club Journal*.

The responsibility for the pictures is recorded in the accompanying List of Illustrations, but I would like to add my appreciation of the special efforts made on my behalf by some of the private photographers whose work I have used. I am grateful to Piero Rossi for the use of a drawing of Fontainebleau and to the editor of *Alpinismus* for providing a copy of it for reproduction.

For advice on isolated points or general assistance with a variety of problems I have to thank in particular:

R. M. Bere, Edward and Diana Bullock, Eric Bunt, John Cleare,

Lt P. S. Cobb, N. Estcourt, L. R. Holliwell, J. Huskins, Harry Pearman and R. H. A. Staniforth.

The libraries of the Alpine Club, the Borough of Richmond upon Thames, the Geological Survey and the Chelsea Speleological Society have been of great help with references and material.

My wife has given the customary sterling help and encouragement at all stages of the project. Christopher and Gillian have also made their contributions.

EDWARD C. PYATT

Hampton
June 1969

PLACE NAME INDEX

Four figure National Grid References are given for all features except those which are very extensive, such as large towns, rivers, bays etc. The reference gives the co-ordinates of the south-west corner of the one kilometre square in which the feature is sited. This simplified co-ordinate system is not unique; every set of four figure co-ordinates is repeated at 100 kilometre intervals both northwards and eastwards, so that the position of a feature must be known within this distance (ie about 60 miles) for the precise location to be found. References to plates are in bold.

K

GENERAL AND PERSONAL INDEX